Questions of Today

SOUTH AFRICA

Allan Leas

B.T. Batsford Ltd, London

Contents

© Allan Leas 1992
First published 1992

Typeset by Tek-Art Ltd Kent
and printed and bound
in Great Britain by
BPCC Hazells Ltd
for the publishers
B.T. Batsford Ltd
4 Fitzhardinge Street
London W1H 0AH

A CIP catalogue record for this book is available from the British Library

ISBN 0 7134 6499 2

Acknowledgments

The Author and Publishers would like to thank the following for permission to reproduce illustrations: Frank Spooner Pictures for pages 3, 10, 25, 27, 28, 30, 51, 52, 55 and 57; International Defence & Aid Fund for pages 4, 6, 8, 9, 13, 14, 22, 24, 29, 32, 34, 36, 39, 40, 42, 46, 48 and 58.

Cover illustration: *Nelson Mandela at a celebration concert following his release from prison in 1990* (courtesy of Rex Features).

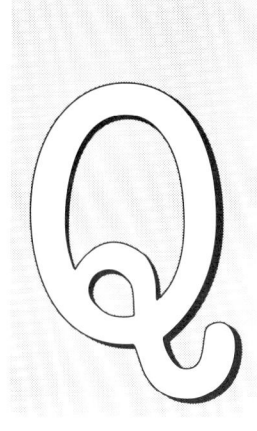

1 South Africa – A New Era?

'The struggle is my life.' Nelson Mandela proved these words by serving 27 years in prison for his beliefs. On his release, he confirmed bringing about the end of apartheid in South Africa and was accepted as the natural choice of leader for the ANC.

On 10 February 1990, Nelson Mandela, by then the world's most famous prisoner, was released.

For several years leading up to his release, the South African white government had been pondering on how to free Mandela, the acknowledged leader of the majority of South Africa's black population. The danger, the whites always feared, was that his release would ignite a revolutionary fire that could not be put out – even by the powerful police force and army that controlled the black townships.

During Mandela's imprisonment, pleas for his release came from both inside and outside South Africa. In an attempt to reply to this pressure, the South African government stated that if Mandela agreed to a number of demands he could walk free. For several years, the government steadfastly insisted that he must give up the 'armed struggle' before his release could be considered. They always knew, however, that Mandela would never

Nelson Mandela and his wife Winnie celebrate together his release from prison.

compromise on his principles in exchange for personal freedom. He had spent 27 years in prison precisely because he had *refused* to bow to the laws of apartheid. It was unlikely that he would give in now. And so the deadlock continued, with no solution in sight. No Afrikaner politician would dare to take the risk of freeing Mandela while he continued to support armed resistance against the white government.

In 1990, F.W. de Klerk, the National Party leader, finally decided to take that risk. He was to free Mandela without further delay. Furthermore, all previous conditions and demands were to be dropped. 'The time for talking has arrived', he announced to a stunned South Africa and a surprised world.

Spontaneous celebrations broke out throughout the black townships of South Africa, as well as in the cities. Archbishop Desmond Tutu, the black Nobel Peace Prize winner and constant government

critic, responded to de Klerk's announcement: 'He has taken my breath away'.

Not only was Mandela to be freed but a new political agenda was put before the white parliament. It stated that 60 banned organizations were to be legalized, including the African National Congress (Mandela's organization) and the South African Communist Party. The remaining major bastions of apartheid were soon to be scrapped. All hangings were to cease until the law on the death penalty had been rewritten.

Within hours of emerging from prison, Mandela was speaking to a crowd of 50,000 cheering people in Cape Town, just a few hundred yards from the white parliament. 'Our resorting to the armed struggle in 1960 was a purely defensive action against the violence of apartheid. We have no option but to continue', he announced.

In that statement, he indicated to his

supporters that he had not compromised with de Klerk for his freedom. Within hours of his release from prison, Mandela insisted on standing firm about the need for armed struggle. His first public speech for 27 years had the effect of confirming the suspicions of many whites who feared that Mandela's release would spark off a revolution. Mandela was worried for another reason. If de Klerk appeared to have gained nothing by freeing Mandela, he might lose his Afrikaner support and be replaced by a more right-wing Afrikaner prime minister. The ANC leader was all too aware of the dangers of pitting his movement against a militant Afrikaner leader, especially at such a key time in their struggle for a democratic South Africa. Mandela told the crowds in Cape Town:

> De Klerk is a man of integrity, and we call on our white compatriots to help us in reshaping a new South Africa. I greet you all in the name of peace, democracy and freedom for all.

This was not a call for a black uprising as some whites had feared, nor did it exclude whites from the future political process. Mandela's statement was a gesture of goodwill that de Klerk, his government and many whites seized gratefully. And so it seemed that the beginnings of a long-sought breakthrough in South Africa's problems had been made. The whites had found a leader (de Klerk) with the courage

FOCUS ON . . . .

South Africa – a snapshot

South Africa is located at the southern tip of the African continent. It is nearly five times the size of the United Kingdom but has less than half the population. The results of the most recent South African government population census (1980) are (in millions): 19.95 'Africans', 4.8 'whites', 2.8 'coloureds' and 0.88 Asians. The whites are separated into two groups, English speakers (1.9 million) and Afrikaners (2.9 million).

The Atlantic Ocean washes the western coastline of South Africa, and the warmer Indian Ocean the eastern coastline. The subtropical location of South Africa and the two oceans result in a climate quite untypical in Africa. It is generally pleasantly warm throughout the country, and in places quite dry. There are occasional droughts, even floods, but the country does not suffer the often extreme climatic conditions of some other African countries.

It has been said on many occasions that South Africa was at war with its neighbours. There have been military invasions, as in the case of South Africa's attack on Angola in 1974, but they were mostly carried out in secret. War was never officially declared. The South African government wanted to weaken the governments and economies of the frontier states. These 'wars' began when the neighbouring countries gained independence from colonial rule. Having just broken free from white rule themselves, they naturally opposed the apartheid regime and gave what support they could to South African anti-apartheid opponents forced into exile.

The countries bordering South Africa are Namibia (date of independence 1990), Botswana (1966), Zimbabwe (1980) and Mozambique (1975). Further north lie Angola (1975), Zambia (1964) and Tanzania (1961), all of which are also considered 'front line' states although they do not border South Africa.

South Africa faced international isolation and boycotts from the 1960s, despite the fact that there were even harsher and less democratic nations in the world. South Africa was singled out by the international community because it, uniquely, made racism the basis of its political system. The system is known as apartheid.

CITY OF DURBAN

UNDER SECTION 37 OF THE DURBAN BEACH BY LAWS, THIS BATHING AREA IS RESERVED FOR THE SOLE USE OF MEMBERS OF THE WHITE RACE GROUP.

STAD DURBAN

HIERDIE GEBIED IS, INGEVOLGE ARTIKEL 37 VAN DIE DURBANSE STRANDVERORDENINGE UITGEHOU VIR DIE UITSLUITLIKE GEBRUIK VAN LEDE VAN DIE BLANKE RASSEGROEP.

This 'whites-only-beach' is one example of many types of racial segregation that existed under the 'petty' apartheid laws. Others were separate cinemas and public transport. The facilities for whites were always of a higher standard than those for blacks.

to acknowledge both the mistakes of the past and the immorality of the apartheid system. The supporters of the ANC had reclaimed their own leader (Mandela), and he had not disappointed them. Nor had he disappointed the expectations of the outside world.

Within months of Mandela's release, several reforms that had previously only been hinted at were being presented to a still surprised, and sometimes shocked, South Africa. A number of the cogs and wheels of the apartheid machine were being removed. Nearly everyone, with the exception of the most unprogressive and conservative whites, welcomed these changes.

One year later, in 1991, most of apartheid legislation was in the process of being scrapped. This included 'petty' apartheid laws as well as 'grand' apartheid laws. 'Petty' laws included such things as beach and park bench segregation. Examples of 'grand' apartheid were the 'homelands' policy and the pass laws (see chapter 2).

However, white minority rule, the backbone of the apartheid system, remained stubbornly in place. All South Africans knew that it was on this single problem that the process of reform could still so easily fail. For over 300 years, whites had dominated political and economic power. This one fact angered black South Africans more than all the apartheid laws put together. Unless blacks and whites could come to an agreement on a fair and democratic transfer of power to the majority of South Africans, de Klerk's gamble was doomed to fail.

Before the coming to power of Prime Minister de Klerk there were strong reasons for Nelson Mandela to be released. Why were previous white prime ministers so reluctant to free him?

After Nelson Mandela's release, did the crisis predicted by the pro-apartheid whites actually occur?

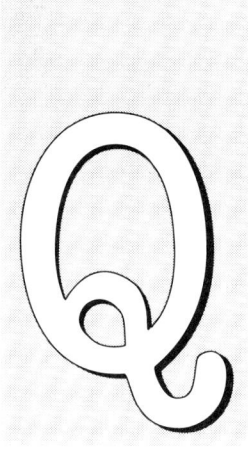

2 300 Years of Minority Rule

This seventeenth-century engraving shows a group of Khoikhoi building huts in the Cape. Their way of life was to be irretrievably devastated by the white settlers.

Many white South Africans continue to believe that their ancestors 'discovered' South Africa in 1652, when a Dutch burgher (citizen), Jan Van Riebeeck, established a permanent refreshment station at the southern tip of Africa.

In fact, the Cape had already been settled for centuries by the San and Khoikhoi (whose societies were nearly wiped out by the white settlers). Nevertheless, many whites still persist in their belief that the Cape was largely devoid of black inhabitants. Because they believe this, they feel that their ancestors were justified in claiming both ownership of the land and political self-determination.

The seventeenth-century Dutch burghers were joined by a group of French Huguenots who were fleeing religious persecution in France. Over the next 200 years, the language they spoke – mostly a dialect of Dutch, but with some French, Portuguese and Malay – evolved into Afrikaans. The people who speak this language are now called the Afrikaners.

In 1820, a group of 5,000 British settlers arrived to farm in the Eastern Cape. They were encouraged to emigrate by the British government in an attempt to balance out the numbers of Britons and Afrikaners in the Cape. British immigrants were humorously described by Afrikaners as *Rooineks* ('Red necks') as they were particularly susceptible to sunburn. These days they are referred to as English-speaking white South Africans.

During the years of white immigration, more and more land was taken from the black peoples. The remaining Khoikhoi and San lost all contact with their previous societies. Many had died of disease and others gradually moved northwards and eastwards, away from white settlements. Many others became the slaves of the whites. There were many intermarriages between the slaves and the whites. The children and descendants of these marriages became known as the 'Cape coloureds'.

This image of the 'Great Trek' shows Boers battling with local Dingaans on their way to their 'promised land'. Many Afrikaners claim to this day that they settled in South Africa before any of the black peoples.

There were nine other major black peoples, or tribes, populating the rest of South Africa. The largest of these groups were the Zulus, Xhosas and Sothos.

The British settlers had the backing of the British government, which by 1814 controlled the Cape Colony. Legislation was soon passed by the British which the Afrikaners did not agree with. The Afrikaners were in particular angered by the repeal of the pass laws which had until then given them the monopoly of black labour by compelling Khoikhoi to work for Afrikaners. Without a pass a Khoikhoi has no right to leave the property of his 'master', who also controlled the issue of passes. Furthermore, in 1834, the British ordered the emancipation of slaves throughout their empire, which included those held by Afrikaners. The Afrikaners

saw this as the final provocation. In 1837, a group of 5,000 Afrikaners left their homes in the Cape and set out on the 'Great Trek' to their 'promised land'. They eventually gained independence from British rule and established the Orange Free State and the Transvaal. These two provinces became the bastions of Afrikaner conservatism and the birth-place of apartheid.

The discovery of diamonds (1870) in the Cape and gold (1886) in the Transvaal attracted a flood of fortune-seeking immigrants from various parts of Europe to South Africa. The Transvaal Afrikaners were horrified by this invasion of *uitlanders* (foreigners, most of whom were British). Soon English-speakers and Afrikaners were at loggerheads again. The discovery of gold and diamonds brought out the worst in both groups. Unrestricted prospecting in the mining industry brought about a sudden turn in South Africa's history.

At first the mines attracted blacks as well as whites. They came from many native kingdoms with the intention of making their fortunes at the diggings. However, the well-armed whites prevented them from doing so. Instead, black men were forced to live in single-sex compounds and their wives and children were kept away. This disrupted traditional black families and societies almost beyond recovery. A massive and landless black working class was created with a speed that had never been seen before. The compounds where the men lived beside the mines were built like prisons. The security arrangements – passes, searches and harsh discipline – that the black workers experienced set the

standard for future industrial legislation. In many ways, the conditions in the mines were reflected in a number of the apartheid laws which were to be introduced later.

The use of labour in the mining industry remained essentially unaltered into the 1990s. The common purpose of the English-speakers and Afrikaners was to exploit cheap black labour. Mining was the mainstay of the white economy. To maintain the unjust master-servant system in the mines required all political power to remain in white hands.

British ambitions were to rule all of southern Africa. To this end an uprising was organized in 1895 by Dr L.S. Jameson. He was a close colleague of Cecil Rhodes, a multi-millionaire who almost single-handedly ran the diamond industry. Between the two of them they came up with a plan to encourage the *uitlanders* to

This photograph, taken in 1985, of miners in their dormitory shows how little living conditions for black workers had changed since the nineteenth century. While miners lived in single-sex compounds their families were left to work the infertile land of the 'homelands'.

Afrikaner soldiers in their *laager* (camp) during the Boer War.

failed to revolt. Rhodes had already spread the story to the British press that the uprising was a spontaneous revolt against the corrupt Kruger regime. As nobody had in fact revolted it became obvious that this was not true. Kruger, the president of the Transvaal republic, responded by rounding up and arresting Jameson's men and sending them to London to be tried.

This attempt by Rhodes to overthrow the elected government of the Transvaal was justifiably seen by the Boers as an imperialist invasion. Tensions continued to heighten. Although the entire incident was of intense embarrassment to the British government, they were still determined to assert authority over both the Transvaal province and the gold mines. They issued a number of demands and ultimatums which the Boers refused to agree to.

The stage was set for war. The British government argued that many of their subjects were disadvantaged by living under the rule of Kruger. These 'subjects' were English-speaking whites, mostly from the United Kingdom, who worked in the mines. In 1899, the British army set sail for the voyage to South Africa. They were eventually to send off nearly half a million soldiers – equal to the entire Afrikaner population. Although the British army had the support of most English-speaking whites, these were not really involved. The fight was between the British army and the Afrikaners (Boers). The Boer War lasted from 1899 to 1902, during which time 26,000 Boer men, women and children died in British concentration camps. Afrikaners continue to refer back to this fact with bitterness.

At the time it was said that it was a 'white man's war'. Nothing could have been further from the truth. Many thousands of blacks were killed during the war, sometimes dying in battle, more often in open massacres.

For the victors, the British, no price seemed too high to persuade the Boers to become British subjects. The Afrikaners had always rejected any proposals that

rebel in such a way that it would appear to be a genuine struggle for political rights in the Transvaal.

Their underlying motive was to wrestle control of the Transvaal from the Boers (the Afrikaners). Rhodes encouraged the *uitlanders* to set up a reform committee in Johannesburg. The aim of the committee was to take control of the Transvaal. Meanwhile, Dr Jameson led a small private army to Johannesburg in support of this committee. The army was to back a pre-arranged uprising of *uitlanders*.

The plan went awry. Jameson's 500 men soon discovered that the *uitlanders* had

British troops in battle. The difference between the two armies was that the British were trained soldiers sent to South Africa especially to fight the war, while the Afrikaners (Boers) were settlers, mainly farmers, protecting the provinces they had established.

their two republics (the Transvaal and the Orange Free State) should be ruled by Britain. A new suggestion was now put forward that all four territories should freely unite. Thus, a new united South Africa comprising the two Afrikaner republics and the two English (the Cape and Natal) would be formed. This was agreed by both sides. And so, the irony of the Boer War was that it finally resulted in South African whites, and particularly the Afrikaners, winning back not only their two republics from the British, but the Cape and Natal as well. This is why it is often said that, although the British won the war, the Afrikaners won the peace. The English-speaking and Afrikaner white South Africans were now planning to bury their differences and rule in unison over the majority black population, with British agreement.

African political associations grouped together to fight this plan for white union, which excluded them from having any political power. These organizations had witnessed the forces of white nationalism at work, which meant suppression for blacks, and were spurred on to resist white domination.

In 1910, the four colonies united to form the Union of South Africa. In September of that year, the South African National Party, led by General Smuts and Louis Botha, won the first general election.

The African National Congress launched their struggle in 1912 (initially called the South African Native National Congress). The following year the Native Land Act was passed. Hundreds of thousands of Africans who had bought land, or were squatting on land in the Transvaal and the Orange Free State,

General Smuts, leader of the National Party. In 1910, he and Louis Botha won the first general election in the united British and Afrikaner South Africa, which excluded blacks from taking any part in the government.

industrial unrest and gloom. The cost of living had shot up, there was a drought and serious crop failures. There were many strikes in response to the worsening standard of living of both black and white workers. In 1918, European workers went on strike at a Johannesburg power station. This action was keenly observed by black 'sanitary workers' at the power station, who were also planning strike action. They, unlike the whites, were subject to the 'Masters and Servants Law', which made their action illegal. They were arrested and imprisoned. The whites, having witnessed this event, were terrified at the idea of African workers organizing a labour movement.

After the First World War, the price of gold fell. The mine owners responded by threatening the jobs of 2,000 white miners whom they intended replacing with cheaper black labour. The white miners organized a massive strike which nearly escalated into a state of civil war in the streets of Johannesburg. General Smuts took the drastic decision to bomb the strikers' headquarters, thus crushing the strike.

An alliance between the Labour Party (against black advancement and for the white strikers) and the National Party led by General J.B.M. Hertzog, won the 1924 general election. Clearly, the Labour Party's support for white workers had paid off. Hertzog now turned to the theme that inspired him most – the rise of the Afrikaner. Unlike Smuts, who had negotiated the union of Afrikaners and British, General Hertzog, an ex-Boer War general, did not see compromise with Britain as a desirable goal. He stated:

> I am not one of those who always have their mouths full of reconciliation . . . South Africa must be governed by the Afrikaner. . . . It can no longer be governed by non-Afrikaners, by people who do not have the right love for South Africa.

were forced off it. The African 'reserves' were offered in compensation. They formed the basis of the 'independent' homelands, which the majority of black people rejected since the time they were introduced. The amount of land set aside for the reserves represented 7.3 per cent of the country. The remaining 92.7 per cent, containing the best land, the mineral wealth and the cities, was for the whites.

The basis for apartheid was now well established. African nationalist forces were growing, as was the African union movement. For all South Africans the years after the war were a period of

During the 1930s, General Hertzog continued to promote Afrikaner commercial and industrial interests. This decade also saw the Afrikaans language, and with it the Afrikaner people, achieve equal official status with English.

By 1934, the country was suffering the economic blight of the depression, which was affecting all industrialized nations. The South African Party (SAP) of General Smuts and the National Party (NP) of General Hertzog merged in an attempt to solve the country's problems. They formed the United Party, led by General Hertzog.

The battle for Afrikaner nationalism was all but won. The ANC had, so far, failed in its bid to effectively resist white domination. Its leadership was split and the white opposition seemed all powerful. It was to take another 50 years before the South African people were to march in mass support of the ANC, waving its flag openly in the streets.

In 1939, Hertzog proposed in Parliament that South Africa should remain neutral in the war against Germany. His proposal was defeated by 80 votes to 67. Hertzog called for a dissolution of Parliament and a general election to finally decide the issue. The Governor-General refused to allow this and invited Smuts to form a new United Party government. General Smuts led South Africa into the Second World War, on the side of the Allies. Many Afrikaners were deeply resentful of the fact that they were once again being asked to spill blood for their past enemy, Britain (as they had done in the First World War).

In 1948, the National Party, now led by Dr D.F. Malan, won the general election. General Smuts suffered a political defeat from which he would never recover. This has come to be known as the 'apartheid election', despite the fact that many of the building blocks of apartheid had been

Dr D.F. Malan (centre) and his cabinet after the 1948 'apartheid election'.

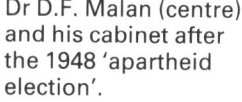

cemented long before this period.

General Smuts, although an ex-Boer soldier, was no longer being identified with the 'purified' Afrikaner struggle. The United Party which he led was not seen by the Afrikaner people as representing their ultimate aspirations. Smuts by then considered himself a world statesman, and to some degree his claim was justified. His support for the Allies during the Second World War was substantial, and for it he received Britain's thanks. His prominence on the world stage was to be his undoing. Smuts lost the 1948 election because he failed to understand that what the Afrikaner people wanted was to take absolute control of the government, to the total exclusion of the English-speakers. They were not about to achieve that aim led by an Afrikaner who spent so much of his time in the 'enemy camp'.

In order to attract the Afrikaner vote, Malan's National Party had openly campaigned on the 'black issue'. The two Afrikaans words that carried most emotional, and electoral, weight amongst the Afrikaner people were *baaskap* and *swart gevaar*. *Baaskap* refers to 'white supremacy' and *swart gevaar* literally means 'black danger'.

When the National Party, led by Dr D.F. Malan, published its 'Race Relations' proposals for this election, they offered the white electorate two options.

> The choice before us is one of these two divergent courses: either that of integration, which would in the long run amount to national suicide on the part of the whites; or that of apartheid, which professes to safeguard the future of every race.

The 'apartheid election' of 1948 was the fulfilment of the Afrikaner nationalists' ultimate dreams. Although Afrikaners had led South Africa for decades, they had never assumed total control of the economy, the civil service and the army and police forces.

Although it is seen as the apartheid election, there are those who argue that apartheid was not the principle aim of the Afrikaner nationalists. Some historians claim that their true intention was finally to take control of South Africa to the exclusion of English-speakers. If that theory is true, the nationalists succeeded totally.

'GRAND' APARTHEID

The 'Afrikaner cause' had intensified, and Smuts' election defeat was due to the fact that he had not quite understood the extent and nature of it. The views of the pro-apartheid voters were summed up in a report prepared to coincide with the 1948 election campaign. It was prepared by a National Party MP, and it stated:

> South Africa's eventual ideal and goal must be total apartheid between whites and blacks.

The report went on to argue the case for black repatriation from the cities to the 'homelands', with the ultimate aim of 'the gradual extraction of natives from industries in white areas'.

These were the policies of 'grand apartheid'. They appealed to poor whites and farmers, but made no sense to industrialists and 'liberal' academics. The capitalists needed to have a black labour force available in the cities. By removing black people from the cities, grand apartheid was threatening industry and enterprise – and the economy would inevitably suffer.

It is possible that not even National Party politicians were fully aware of the monumental development in politics that they were bringing about. For many years, racist laws had been passed individually. Now, all these laws were about to be brought together into the single ideology of apartheid. This ideology was so clear cut, systematic and uncompromising in its practice that it could be clearly distinguished from almost any other forms of racism that occurred in the rest of the world. (And because of that, it was universally criticized.)

Some people who tried to justify

apartheid argued that the system was designed to protect the rights of 'all minorities'. They said that black South Africans were divided into 'tribes', each of which, like the whites, was a minority. The validity of the 'minorities' rights and 'tribal' excuses for apartheid were exaggerated out of all proportion. In response, opponents of apartheid refused to acknowledge any references to differences in tribe, language and cultural background when these groupings were used to divide South Africans.

Anti-apartheid voices understood only too well that if all of South Africa's black people rejected the concept of separate rights for separate groups, then the remaining *ideological* argument, used by the whites for the continuence of an apartheid system, would disappear.

The National Party were ready to put into practice the promises that had won them the general election. And these promises contained unimaginable consequences for the blacks. Each black 'tribe' was to have its own 'homeland' – whether they liked it or not. And every 'African' South African was to be a citizen of 'their' homeland. It was a crude but devastating method of creating a controlled migrant labour force. Blacks were prevented from going to the cities without permission, and permission could only be gained when they were needed to work. Once in the cities, blacks were regarded as foreigners in a white country and could be 'repatriated' to the homelands at any time. The creation of homelands simultaneously provided an illusion of democracy for black people as they were supposedly self-governing within their own homelands – which were, of course, in the least fertile land without mineral deposits. The National Party policy document stated clearly the status blacks would have:

> Blacks in urban areas should be regarded as migratory citizens not entitled to political or social rights equal to those of the whites.

In 1948, none of these policies was novel. But they were now being presented as the only path for the survival of South Africa's whites. The Afrikaners knew that, in the longer term, *baaskap* could not be maintained unless black aspirations were totally suppressed. Grand apartheid could do this.

THE 'THREAT' OF BLACK INDUSTRIAL POWER

The increasing support for the National Party cannot be explained solely in terms of the conflict between English-speakers and Afrikaners. Nor can it be explained solely by the attraction of the Afrikaner electorate to the uninhibited promises of *baaskap* rule.

Leading up to the Second World War, the number of African workers in the manufacturing industries had increased from 76,000 to 249,000. During the war, because of the white call-up, many of these Africans were moved into semi-skilled work. A government commission had earlier warned that by creating a black working class it 'would inevitably result in class war'.

The Board of Trade and Industry warned in 1945 of the dangers of:

> the detribalization of large numbers of natives congregated in . . . masses in large industrial centres.

As women discovered in Britain during the two world wars, so too Africans discovered in South Africa during the Second World War that they had industrial muscle. During the period of the war itself, there were 304 strikes by mainly African workers.

These strikes were proving many white supporters of apartheid correct. Their worst fears about the black working class were beginning to materialize. During the war, General Smuts and his United Party had been forced to make concessions to African workers. Very soon, their wages began to increase. Encouraged by their successes, the black workers began to make more demands. The whites were made aware of the threat this posed to their power.

The farmers were moving *en masse* towards the hard-line apartheid policies of the National Party. At the time, 84 per cent of white farmers were Afrikaners. There were about 800,000 whites living on farms and they represented about 30 per cent of the white population. Their political influence was therefore quite considerable.

Manufacturing industry was moving in a different direction – it was desperate for skilled black labour and a larger home market to stimulate demand for goods. English-speaking industrialists had begun to recognize that the African workers could not in the longer term be 'contained'. They had to be appeased, and one method was to 'give them a stake in the capitalist economy'.

The National Party leaders bought none of it. They believed that industrial reform would result in more demands being made and eventually in revolution. For them, the long-term implications appeared dangerous, both for continued white supremecy and for the survival of capitalism.

Now in power, the leaders of the National Party were free at last to implement 'grand' apartheid. Parliament immediately set about passing several pieces of apartheid legislation which provided the foundations of the system. These were the Mixed Marriages Act, the Population Registration Act, the Suppression of Communism Act and the Group Areas Act. In 1952, another act was passed. It was called the Abolition of Passes and Co-ordination of Documents Act. Despite the misleading title, it was in reality the introduction of the despised pass system, which aimed to control the movement of all black South Africans.

Most of the apartheid legislation from this period had, by 1990, either been replaced, amended or done away with. Thankfully, the following definitions of the planks of apartheid can be read as history.

THE MIXED MARRIAGES ACT

This act made marriages between 'Europeans' and 'non-Europeans' a criminal offence. It was an extension of another act called the 'Immorality Act', which made it illegal for 'illicit carnal intercourse' between black and white. This act was unpopular with very many white South Africans, as well as black – for obvious reasons. Both these Acts have now been abolished.

THE POPULATION REGISTER ACT

This act was introduced in 1950. On face value, it does not appear to be controversial, as most countries compile a register of their populations and issue identification papers.

In South Africa, though, this Act took on a very different character. People were classified into three distinct groups: 'white', 'coloured' and 'native'. To be a white person in South Africa was considered by them to be a 'privilege' (because, in real terms, it *bought* many privileges). For generations, there were people of mixed race who had succeeded in entering the 'white' group. Quite suddenly, they were forced by law to sort themselves out according to race. Many who had been previously accepted as 'white' were re-classified 'coloured'. Families were split. Children of the same parents were separated, some classified 'white', others 'coloured'. About 100,000 people appealed against their classification. Many lost their jobs or were forced to move home. Those who chose to remain married to a partner who had a different classification were liable to arrest. Many suicides resulted, and many married couples were separated.

For the hundreds of thousands of blacks who had immigrated into South Africa, often marrying and settling with families, the tragedy was even greater. They were not included in the population register. This designated them as official aliens, liable to deportation at any moment. It proved to be a powerful method of controlling the influx and movement of very many black people.

The court appeals often ended in tragic farce when the classifications of a person could not be decided. Fingernails were examined. Combs were even pulled through hair:

> If the comb is halted by tight curls the person is more likely to be classified coloured.

Example case

In 1981, a woman was arrested for residing in a 'white' area. She lived in a suburb of Johannesburg. The magistrate convicted her because he considered her to be 'coloured'. He did so on the basis of her having 'a flat nose, wavy hair, a pale skin and high cheekbones'.

The case went to the Supreme Court. The judges finally ruled in her favour, declaring: 'While the woman was not obviously white she was generally accepted as such.'

There were countless similiar cases in the courts. The disruption of lives and entire families were in the hands of judges – and the criteria they employed to classify people never had any scientific basis. There were in fact 'no hard and fast rules'. A leading world expert was asked to provide a hair classification for 'coloured' people. His reply was quite straightforward: 'There isn't one'.

THE SUPPRESSION OF COMMUNISM ACT

This act declared the Communist Party to be an unlawful organization. All other parties, organizations or persons who promoted 'communistic activities' were also declared illegal.

The act was used to stifle almost any government opposition. The definition of 'communism' was extremely wide, including 'any related form of that doctrine'. Arguing for world peace, trade union internationalism and the end of colonialism could all be considered by the courts to be related forms of communism, punishable by ten years imprisonment. Strikes which did not fall within the provisions of the

Industrial Conciliation Act might be deemed an 'unlawful act', under the definition of communism.

This piece of legislation was also used as a means to 'ban' people. A banning order is a document signed by the Minister of Law and Order which controls the movement of the banned person, and prevents him or her from speaking publicly or being quoted. Banning or house arrest was often used to silence critics of the government when there was not enough evidence to convict the person in a court of law. The ANC President, Albert Luthuli, was banned on the grounds 'that he was a communist'. He was, in fact, a Christian anti-communist (and winner of the Nobel peace prize). Nelson Mandela was also at one stage banned under this act, 'as a communist'.

In 1966, the Minister of Justice, B.J. Vorster (later to become prime minister), finally admitted:

> You don't have to be a communist to be banned under the Suppression of Communism Act.

Several members of the Liberal Party of South Africa were also banned under this act, despite being strongly anti-communist. Hundreds of others who were not communists were also banned. The reply to these people was always the same:

> You were banned because in the opinion of the minister you were furthering the aims of communism.

Example case

Terence Beard, a university lecturer, was banned in 1964. One day, he attended a party given by a colleague. According to his banning order, he was not allowed to be in the same room as more than one other person – otherwise it would constitute a 'gathering'. And so he remained throughout the night in the kitchen. If fellow party-goers wanted to see him, they came in one at a time. Nevertheless, the police entered the house and arrested him, charging him with breaking his banning order. Although he had determined not to be in the company of more than one person at any time, he was found guilty on the grounds that the other party-goers had a 'common purpose' (i.e. to 'party').

THE PASS LAWS

The pass laws, of all the measures that black people had to suffer under, were the most loathsome. The 'pass' system had long been introduced, but in this new form it was to prove to be even harsher in its implementation. Every 'African' was forced to carry a pass. This pass regulated every minute of his or her life, their movements, their place of work and their place of residence. At any time, a policeman could demand to see the pass, and failure to produce it more often than not resulted in a heavy fine or imprisonment. The effect of this law was to 'criminalize' a large section of South African black people.

It was stated in September 1985 that the total number of Africans arrested between 1916 and 1981 was 17.12 million. The heaviest sentence for not having a pass was 250 days in prison. In 1982, when asked what the frequency of arrests were in South Africa under the pass laws, Parliament was told, 'one person every two and a half minutes'.

Example case

Efforts by South African sporting bodies to return to the international arena received many setbacks. Anti-apartheid groups always argued that eliminating apartheid in sports stadiums was no reason to lift the boycott. Their case was strengthened when a leading black road runner, Epraim Sibisi, was arrested by five policemen for not carrying a pass. The absurdity of expecting an athlete to carry identification papers with him turned from farce into near tragedy when on the night of his arrest he was assaulted in his cell. Despite his status as an athlete, he had become one of the 17 million criminalized and humiliated by the pass system.

THE GROUP AREAS ACT

The Group Areas Act of 1950 was also known as the 'Ghetto Act'. Once again, it separated the population into three racial groups: white, coloured (which includes Asians) and Africans. Areas were proclaimed for the exclusive occupation of a particular group: 'no member of any one group may occupy or own land in the proclaimed area of another'. The immediate result of this act was the mass uprooting of entire communities of Indian, 'coloured' and African people. Sometimes these communities were forcibly moved from land on which they had resided for centuries.

This act was another example of grand apartheid. The National Party, leading up to the 1948 election, had attracted the support of many 'poor white' voters. These people often lived in 'mixed' areas, and were keen to see coloured people forced out. The Group Areas Act had the desired effect, and the party's election promises were fulfilled. The National Party had repaid its debt to its electorate.

In 1985, the government released some figures for the number of people forcibly moved from their homes: 126,176 families. Of those, 66 per cent were coloured, 32 per cent Indian and 2 per cent white.

The chairman of the right-wing South African Bureau for Racial Affairs stated that allowing people of different races to live side by side would be 'tantamount to national suicide'. In 1986, the State President stated that the act was 'the cornerstone' of minority rights in South Africa.

There was large-scale opposition to this law, including opposition from the churches (but not the Afrikaner Dutch Church). In response, the Prime Minister, Dr Malan, told church leaders that they shouldn't question him, but God.

Why did the Creator make the mistake of creating countries, nations and languages? He should not have done so . . . and in addition the Creator also proceeded to create different colours. I say that [opposition to the Group Areas

Sport

Before the sports boycotts, the all-white South African cricket and rugby teams were highly rated internationally. White South Africans were very proud of their successful teams and it was this pride that made them vulnerable to the attack of anti-apartheid campaigners. When South African sports were boycotted white South Africans were deeply hurt. Without any doubt, it was a well-aimed and highly successful anti-apartheid strategy. In 1963, the International Olympic Committee informed South Africa that unless racial discrimination was eliminated from sport they would not be invited to the next games. Verwoerd, the Prime Minister, refused the suggestion, and South Africa was out of the Olympics.

The arrogance of apartheid meant that it did not only apply to South African sportsmen and women, but to visiting teams as well. There are numerous examples. Maoris were banned from being included in a New Zealand rugby team in 1961. The 'coloured' cricketer Basil d'Oliveira, could not play as a member of the visiting English cricket team in 1968. Colin Croft, a West Indian cricketer, was ordered off a 'white' train in 1983.

Until 1976, official government policy was that all sport should, as far as possible, be segregated. Finally the international boycotts began to affect the government's attitude, and sports apartheid was relaxed. By 1991, segregation in sport had just about been eradicated. The international community responded by allowing the new 'non-racial' South African sporting bodies to enter the world sports arena. Many anti-apartheid protesters continued to argue against this. They used the following facts as evidence that 'apartheid' still existed in sports: although whites were a minority, white schools had 72% of all sports facilities; whites owned 73% of all athletic tracks, 83% of swimming pools and 82% of rugby fields.

In 1991, the fact remained that the apartheid system had created such economic hardships for black people that simply removing the policy of segregation would not be enough to 'normalize' sport in South Africa. Sport was so much a part of South African life, on so many levels, that removing discrimination from it entirely would prove just as difficult as scrapping apartheid itself.

Act] is a charge against Creation and the Creator.

By 1990, the Group Areas Act was still in existence. For the black people in South Africa, and in the eyes of the outside world, apartheid was still operating, although there was strong talk of the act being 'reformed'. The danger for the National Party in scrapping the act was the inevitable loss of hard-line Afrikaner support to the Conservative Party and to the far right. The gains in scrapping the act would be the advancement of negotiations with black nationalist groups, and the support of English-speaking, white anti-apartheid voters. In 1991 the Group Areas Act was finally scrapped.

How did the Afrikaans language evolve?

Many white South Africans say that their claims to most of South Africa are historical and fair. Is this true?

Are all white South Africans called Afrikaners?

Who are the 'Cape coloured' people?

Why did the abolition of slavery in 1834 throughout the British Empire so anger the Afrikaners?

What effect did the discovery of gold and diamonds have on the relationship between English-speaking and Afrikaans-speaking South Africans?

Did the outcome of the Boer War result in an improved situation for black South Africans?

It is often said that apartheid began in 1948 when the National Party came to power. Is this true?

When the African National Congress was established, what were its first methods of protest?

General Smuts was a world statesman and a war hero. Why then was he voted out of power so soon after the end of the Second World War?

Afrikaner farmers were strong supporters of apartheid. Yet those controlling manufacturing industry felt that rigid apartheid policies were not entirely in the interests of free market capitalism. Why did the two groups differ?

How did the pass laws affect the average black South African?

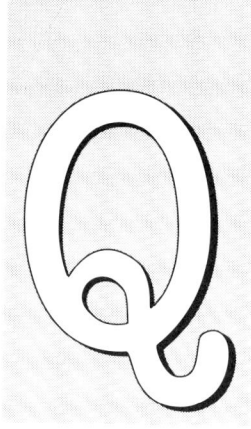

3 Nelson Mandela and the Black Nationalist Struggle

On 21 March 1960, crowds assembled at Sharpeville to protest against the pass laws. What began as a peaceful demonstration ended in the murder of 69 demonstrators by the police.

During my lifetime I have dedicated my life to the struggle of the African people. I have fought against white domination, and I have fought against black domination. I have cherished the ideal of a democratic and free society in which all persons live together in harmony and with equal opportunities. It is an ideal which I hope to live for, and see realized. But my Lord, if needs be, it is an ideal for which I am prepared to die.

That was part of Nelson Mandela's final statement in court during the Rivonia Trial of 1963. Twelve others were charged with Mandela with 'acts of sabotage and damage to property'.

At this time, the Sharpeville massacre of 69 people was fresh in the minds of all South Africans. The shooting by the police of so many black people was the result of a peaceful demonstration against the pass laws. The horrific incident was the cul-

FOCUS ON . . . .

Sharpeville

The Sharpeville massacre on 21 March 1960 was a landmark in both anti-apartheid resistance and government oppression. Over the years, thousands of people have died as a result of apartheid policies, but the tragic death of 69 people at Sharpeville finally exposed to the world the inhuman nature of the regime.

This is what happened. Sharpeville had been a so-called 'model' township. Construction began in 1942. It was near Vereeniging, about 50 miles south of Johannesburg. It boasted neat houses, running water and sanitation, and for 20 years there was no political violence. Many people had voluntarily moved there from the old, overcrowded township nearby. Finally in 1959, the building work was completed. Then, quite suddenly, the remaining inhabitants of the old township were told that they would have to move to Sharpeville, whether they liked it or not. Five thousand people resisted, claiming that they could not afford the high rents. They were all physically evicted to the 'reserves'. This was the first incident in a series of government provocations.

The area was known for its steel manufacturing, and many factory owners preferred their workers to live in company compounds. These compounds had a total population of 11,000, mostly migrant workers from the 'reserves' who were on short-term contracts. Young people who lived in Sharpeville were not as easy to control as the migrant workers in the compounds, and many of them had difficulty finding jobs. Then, in response to the pass laws, the Pan African Congress organized a demonstration outside the local police station. Five thousand protesters joined the demonstration. By quarter past one that night the crowds were still there. The police was unable to disperse them and waited nervously behind a wire fence, as reinforcements continued to arrive. Finally a scuffle broke out and a policeman was pushed over. The crowd surged forwards to see what had happened. Some young constables panicked and began to fire. The crowd turned and ran, scattering in all directions. One hundred and eighty people were wounded. Sixty-nine died, nearly all of whom were shot in the back.

The world reaction was immediate. The intense anger both in South Africa and around the world about apartheid erupted overnight. Strikes and demonstrations against apartheid became widespread. The economy almost collapsed, house prices plummeted and foreign investment halted. The government responded with more repressive measures than ever before. The ANC and PAC were banned; 18,000 people were arrested; and a state of emergency was announced. The apartheid regime had shown its true colours but had also cut itself off from the rest of the world forever.

mination of protests that had continued throughout the 1950s, and is still seen as a crucial milestone in anti-apartheid resistance. A state of emergency soon followed the angry outcry that resulted from the massacre. Adding to the gloom of this time were the facts that the African National Congress and the Pan African Congress had been banned and that the economy was in a bad way. The political atmosphere was justifiably described as 'oppressive'. Mandela had been frustrated at every turn. All peaceful means of protest had been denied his fellow black South Africans. In December 1961, the ANC finally announced that it now had no option but to adopt violent methods to make its protest heard.

Mandela's statement to the judge was not apologetic. Those South Africans who continued to support the ANC were desperately afraid for Mandela and the other accused. One of the defence team, George Bizos focused sharply on the essence of those anxieties: 'The death sentence loomed large'.

Eight of the accused in the Rivonia Trial. Top, left to right: Nelson Mandela, Walter Sisulu, Govan Mbeki, Raymond Mhlaba; bottom: Elias Motsoaledi, Andrew Mlangeni, Ahmed Kathrada, Dennis Goldberg.

How was the judge going to respond to the defendant's insistance on justifying the ANC's decision to move away from peaceful protest? Mandela's speech from the dock was described as 'a forthright heroic statement'. But it was provocative to a white judge who expected to hear statements of apology and pleas for mercy. George Bizos was unable to offer hope or comfort to the accused, in particular to Mandela. 'What do you say to a man who says "I am prepared to die for what I believe in and for what I want"', he commented.

Meanwhile, the outside world was closely monitoring the trial. The United Nations in particular was clear in its response. On 10 October 1963, the UN passed a resolution by 106 votes to 1, calling for the release of the accused in the Rivonia Trial. Thereafter, that date was dedicated as the Day of Political Prisoners.

The country was preparing itself for the sentence. Many white South Africans must have had mixed feelings about the court's findings. To sentence Mandela and his fellow accused to death could have possibly ignited an unknown internal response, as well as world condemnation. Black South Africans, however, were clear about their own feelings. George Bizos summed up the effect Mandela's speech had made on them:

> I think he touched a chord in the hearts and minds of the majority of black people in South Africa. It is possibly one of the reasons why he has acquired the status he has now.

For all the praise, and criticism, of Nelson Mandela's actions leading up to the trial and beyond, no one doubted his status as a leader. Some might argue that by nature of his birth, being the son of a chief, he was destined to assume the role of leader. Others point out that Mandela was both a victim and witness to the miseries brought about by apartheid, and was driven solely by this experience.

Nelson Rolihlahla Mandela was born on 18 July 1918 in Transkei. After completing his schooling, Mandela enrolled for a BA degree at Fort Hare College, then a fertile and active environment for black politics and dissent. Soon, displaying his leadership qualities, he was elected to the students representative council before joining a student boycott which resulted in his suspension from the college. He then set off for Johannesburg, where he established contact and friendships with ANC members. The mines were the obvious place to seek employment in Johannesburg. Mandela's first job, ironically, was as a compound policeman, during which time he was equipped with a knobkerrie (a stick weapon) and a whistle.

Nelson Mandela in Xhosa costume. Born in the Transkei region, Mandela was a member of the Tembu ruling family, and was exposed to black politics from an early age.

Mandela lived in Soweto with Walter Sisulu, one of the leaders of the ANC. Sisulu encouraged him to complete his BA degree and to study law. In 1944 Mandela formally joined the ANC. Together with several other ANC members, he helped to form the Youth League. This organization within the ANC was determined to rejuvenate the movement and establish a united, coherent and spirited opposition to the white regime. The Youth League was known as 'the brains trust and power station of the spirit of African Nationalism'. The idea of foreign leadership or outside ideologies were rejected as contrary to the concept of African Nationalism. The Youth League initially took a strong anti-communist stance as communism was a European concept.

Mandela's rise through the ranks of the ANC was rapid. By now, it was clearly beginning to develop as the central force of resistance to white minority rule. Significantly, it achieved notable success in attracting the support of the South African Indian Congress. This brought two significant black peoples together.

The 'coloured' people, mostly in the Cape, had until then strong ethnic and political ties to the whites. To break these ties and bring the coloured people under the black nationalist umbrella was a task Mandela and the ANC had set themselves. The introduction of the Population Registration Act helped enormously. Many coloured people who had previously been accepted as white were now being reclassified. Together with reclassification, many of the other new apartheid laws weighed in against them. A large proportion of this community was beginning to realize that the answer to their problems was not to attempt to align with the whites, but with the blacks. Many now joined the ANC. Africans, Indians and coloureds were now forming into a single force, about to launch a resistance drive now known as the Defiance Campaign.

The introduction of the Suppression of Communism Act once again acted to unify resistance to apartheid. Not only were differing cultural and racial groups beginning to work together, but so too were people of different political philosophies. There were approximately 1,500 members in the Communist Party at that time, most of whom were still committed to political action. Now that they were banned, many of them now saw the ANC as the only effective force to continue their campaign. Many joined the ANC, together with other whites who were non-communist.

The ANC, with Indian, coloured and some white support, began to demand the repeal of six particularly unjust laws. Mandela was appointed national volunteer-in-chief of the Defiance Campaign. He travelled the length and breadth of South Africa preparing for the long struggle ahead. A letter was drafted and sent to Malan, the prime minister, stating that if there was not a repeal of this legislation the defiance campaign would begin. In the letter, it was pointed out that the ANC had attempted every constitutional method to achieve a change in attitude to the African people, but to no avail. Among the six laws they wanted removed were the Pass Laws, the Group Areas Act, the Suppression of Communism Act, and the Separate Representation of Voters Act. Malan refused to listen or talk to them. Instead, he instructed his secretary to inform them that if they defied the law the government would:

> make full use of the machinery at its disposal to quell any disturbances and deal adequately with those responsible for initiating subversive activity.

Mandela had agreed that the campaign should be non-violent. Each act of defiance was carefully planned, its participants instructed not to resist arrest nor to retaliate violently. The ANC set out to try these tactics on the white police force. Mandela and other ANC leaders believed that if enough blacks refused to comply with the apartheid laws the prisons would

TREASON TRIAL

The
ACCUSED

DECEMBER
1956

The 156 accused in the Treason Trial of 1956. Mandela is in the centre of the third row.

The government was worried by these incidences of black resistance. In December 1952, they decided to arrest the leaders of the Defiance Campaign. Nelson Mandela, Walter Sisulu and 18 others were arrested under the Suppression of Communism Act and tried for leading the campaign. The accused had been so public in their call for non-violent action that even the judge could not help but state, finally, that the charges:

> had nothing to do with communism as it is commonly known. I accept the evidence that you have consistently advised your followers to follow a peaceful course of action and to avoid violence in any shape or form.

Twenty leaders were given nine-month suspended sentences for organizing the campaign. Mandela was one of those 20. During the Defiance Campaign of 1952, the role that Mandela had played so impressed the ANC membership that he was elected president of the Transvaal organization. A high price was soon to be paid for his work. Mandela was served a banning order which prohibited him from attending gatherings and confined him to Johannesburg. It was already clear that Mandela's commitment to his peoples struggle would entail personal sacrifices, all of which he was well prepared to accept. There followed a series of new arrests and trials, until 1956 when he faced the most serious charge yet, treason.

Mandela was accused and charged with 'treason' and promoting communism. There were 155 people charged alongside him. The trial was to last from 1956 to 1961, then laying claim to being the longest in history. The ANC was in the dock, and its policies were under scrutiny. The court case was soon to reveal Mandela's skill as a speaker. The prosecution were determined to prove that he was both a communist and a revolutionary. Mandela's astonishing replies to the prosecution's accusations ran to 440 pages. They revealed much about his thinking and the breadth of his vision for a

soon overflow, and it would become plain that the system was both illogical and unmanageable.

One evening, Mandela and a group of 50 others walked through the Johannesburg streets after 11 pm. This was a white area, and they had broken the evening curfew, which required that all blacks be off the streets by 11 o'clock. They were soon arrested. This was an example of the type of defiance action that Mandela and the ANC had planned. Others soon took up this example.

Nelson and Winnie Mandela at their wedding on 14 June 1958. They were to spend nearly all of their married life apart.

new South Africa. Here is an excerpt from the trial:

Prosecution: Has the ANC considered whether the white supremacy in South Africa would, without a show of arms, offer a surrender of power that would mean its end?

Mandela: We will force the whites by using our numbers, to grant us what we demand, even against their will. We considered that and we felt that that was possible. We worked on the basis that Europeans themselves, in spite of the wall of prejudice and hostility which we encountered, cannot remain indifferent to our demands, because we are hitting them in the stomach with our policy of economic pressure. It is a method which is well organized.

Prosecution: But isn't your freedom a direct threat to the Europeans?

Mandela: No, it is not a direct threat to the Europeans. We are not anti-white, we are against white supremacy, and

In 1961, the Umkhonto we Sizwe (MK) was formed as the armed wing of the ANC, which had by now been banned and had gone underground. The soldiers of the MK were trained in exile (as shown in this photograph) before infiltrating back in to South Africa to carry out acts of sabotage. For example, in June 1980, the MK attacked the state-owned oil company SASOL causing millions of Rands worth of damage.

have the support of some sections of the European population. We have consistently preached a policy of race harmony and we have condemned racialism no matter by whom it is professed.

Following the trial, Mandela was soon to prove to be the ANC's most valued leader.

Winnie Mandela, his second wife, met him during the Treason Trial. She recalled:

> I knew when we were married that our life wouldn't be normal and that he could be jailed. As I grew to love him I understood his kind of life – that it wasn't a normal kind of life. Marrying him was not really marrying the man ... I was marrying the struggle.

Although Mandela was eventually acquitted on the charge of treason, he knew that his freedom was going to be short lived. He returned home from the court accompanied by the leadership of the ANC. Joe Modise, one of those leaders, walked into Mandela's house and told Winnie that Nelson wanted one set of clothing. Mandela remained outside. He wouldn't enter the house, even to say farewell. He took the clothes and went off. The next Winnie heard about him was that he had made a speech to the all-Africa conference in Maritzburg. After that, he disappeared. This was the start of his journey of resistance to liberate his people which was to lead inevitably to life imprisonment. Nelson Mandela had gone underground.

By 1961, Mandela had been dubbed the 'Black Pimpernel'. In that same year, he left on a secret mission overseas, visiting the heads of states of many African countries. He also made a trip to Britain. His task was to gather support for the

ANC, and to that end he was extremely successful.

Life on the road came to an end on 5 August 1962, when he was caught at a police road-block. He was tried and sentenced to five years in prison (three for incitement and two for leaving the country illegally). As he left the court on the way to prison there were shouts of *amandla ngawethu* (power to the people). His wife, Winnie Mandela, was on the pavement among the crowds, who broke into the unofficial national anthem, *Nkosi Sikelele i'Afrika*. (God Save Africa). Soon after this trial, he found himself taken from prison and put back in court, this time fighting for his life.

Those were the events leading up to the Rivonia Trial. In the trial Mandela was accused of taking part in deliberate acts of violence against the state. By now,

Mandela had come to the conclusion that selected acts of sabotage were the only way to put pressure on the government to change. Peaceful protest alone, he now believed, had not worked. Mandela and the other accused waited for the judge to deliberate on the sentence. Dr Percy Yutar, the prosecutor in the trial, acknowledged that those on trial were not personally responsible for any of the acts they were accused of:

> It is tragic to think that the accused, who between them did not have the courage to commit a single act of sabotage themselves, should have incited their followers to acts of sabotage and guerrilla warfare, armed insurgency, open rebellion and ultimately civil war.

This statement was a gross injustice to the

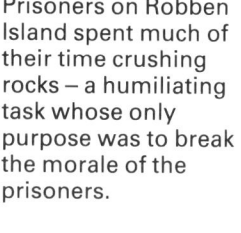

Prisoners on Robben Island spent much of their time crushing rocks – a humiliating task whose only purpose was to break the morale of the prisoners.

accused. They were all men who were prepared to die for both the decisions and actions they took. Even though an apology to the court and a plea for mercy might have lessened their sentences, they stood bravely together, ready to pay the supreme sacrifice. The prosecutor's accusation of cowardice fell on deaf ears.

When the judge, Justice de Wet, finally rose he announced that he was not going to impose the death sentence. Naturally this came as a great relief to the accused, their families and all their supporters. Mandela was sentenced to life imprisonment. In South Africa this life term meant precisely life.

The prisoners' lawyer, George Bizos, asked whether their wives and children could be given the opportunity to say goodbye. With a completely straight face Colonel Aucamp replied: 'Of course the wives and children must be given the opportunity to say goodbye'. When they arrived at the prison they were turned away and told that it was too late, the prisoners had already been taken to Robben Island.

Quite simply known as 'The Island' to its prisoners, Robben Island lies a few miles away from Cape Town, the parliamentary capital of South Arica and the historical port of arrival for most white settlers. It was virtually impossible to escape from Robben Island: even if a prisoner managed to break free from the prison itself, he would still have somehow to cross ten kilometres of shark-infested sea to Cape Town on the mainland.

Ahmed Kathrada, one of those sentenced to the Island with Mandela, explains how the prison authorities managed to introduce apartheid into prison routine:

> Africans used to get porridge in the morning and evening, and corn in the afternoon. Coloureds and Indians got porridge in the morning, samp in the afternoon with bread. The quantity of meat was also different. Coloureds and Indians had more than Africans.

This attempt to create divisions between the prisoners of different racial and cultural backgrounds failed. Mandela and his fellow prisoners mixed all their food and shared it out equally.

Mandela was initially held in a cell called the 'zinc trunk'. It was described by another prisoner:

> Very cold. A hard surface. The accoustics very very good. Under perpetual guard. The lights remaining on throughout the night.

Newspapers were banned. Prisoners caught with newspapers were sent to isolation cells. They often did this on purpose to pass on information they had read to prisoners living in that section.

Much of Mandela's time was spent in a courtyard breaking stones. Raymond Mhlaba, an ex-prisoner, describes the frustration of this task:

> There was no purpose in breaking stones. It was just a humiliating thing to do because you break stones into small particles and they say 'that's not the size we want'. Then you would aim for a certain size until you just gave up.

Nelson Mandela met his lawyer, Ismail Ayob, for the first time in 1972. Ayob had been given permission to meet his client on the Island. He described his meeting with Mandela as 'memorable':

> He was striding down a gentle slope with two young white warders trying to keep up with him at half a sprint. He introduced me to them by their first names.
>
> He felt guilty that he had been a bad father and a bad husband. Most husbands and fathers have taken care of their families and saw their children growing up. Because of the choice he had made – that the people come first – he had had to sacrifice his family.

Finally, after many years, Mandela was taken from Robben Island and transferred to a prison on the mainland. By 1985, his reputation as a leader had grown into

Nelson Mandela's supporters never stopped demonstrating for his release throughout his 27 years in prison. These 'Free Mandela' demonstrators who marched to Pollsmoor Prison in Cape Town, where he was held from 1985, were attacked by the police.

almost mythical proportions. Although cut off from the world for decades, he had somehow managed to create the impression of a political figure who was the key to the South African problem. The two demands that the world community insisted on were the dismantling of apartheid and the release of Nelson Mandela. In some ways the two began to mean the same thing. Isolated from the world for so long, few people knew quite what to expect of him. Intrigue and mystery about Mandela served to feed the huge expectations that the world had laid on his shoulders. Even his image became the focus of world attention. Television companies and newspapers commissioned artists to attempt impressions of what Mandela might look like since he had last been photographed nearly 30 years previously. A nurse who treated him was offered one million rand (about £200,000) for a photograph.

In 1985, in his new prison in Cape Town, Mandela was allowed to meet Professor Samual Dash from the United States.

He appeared vigorous and healthy, with a calm, confident manner and dignified bearing that seemed incongruous in the prison surroundings. Indeed, throughout our meeting, I felt I was in the presence not of a guerilla fighter or radical idealogue, but of a head of state.

By December 1988, it was clear to all that the government was preparing to release Mandela. He was transferred to another prison complex, and was given a warder's house to live in, complete with swimming pool. Mandela knew that his years as a prisoner were soon to end. All that was required by the government was a face-saving way to release him. Mandela was not about to offer it, forcing President de Klerk finally to make the decision anyway, and face the consequences.

In December 1961, the ANC announced a change of tactic. What was decided and how did the white regime react?

What were the main demands of the ANC during the Defiance Campaign of 1952?

Why was the white government so determined to convict the leaders of the ANC? What were the whites' real fears?

How did Nelson Mandela manage to attain the status of a world figure from a tiny prison cell on Robben Island? What were his 'special' qualities that drew so much respect?

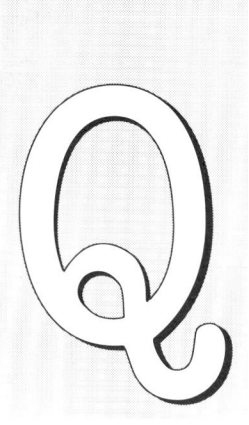

4 Biko and Black Consciousness

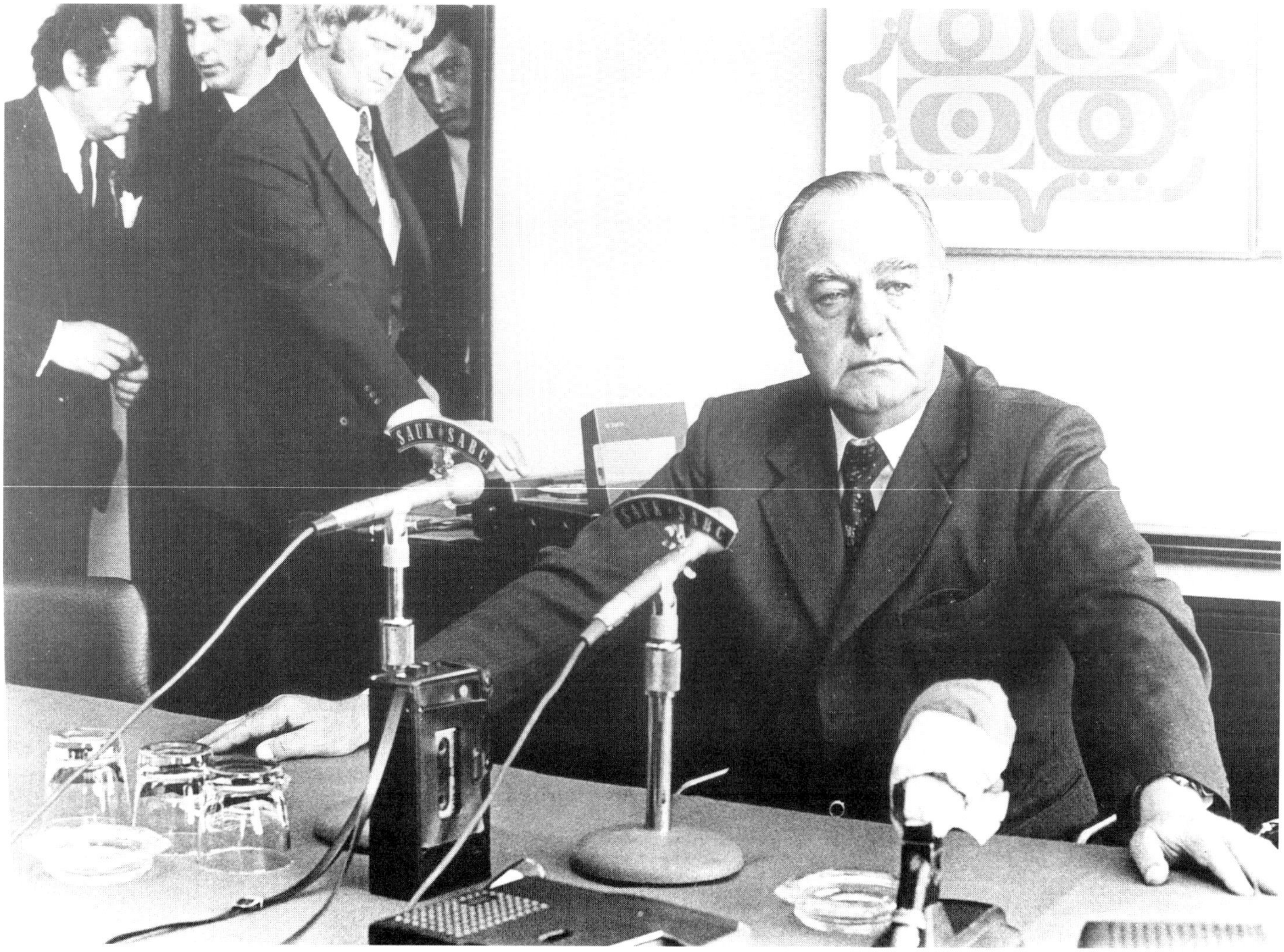

The South African prime minister in 1977 was B.J. Vorster. His period of office can be remembered for the millions of people he deported to the homelands, for reinforcing police powers, and for the Soweto riots in 1976 (see page 39). In addition to this legacy of oppression, his term of office witnessed another major political mistake. On 12 September 1977, yet another detainee had died in police custody. Since Vorster had been put in charge of the Ministry of Justice, 45 detainees had died in police 'care'. The majority, the police claimed, had committed suicide – by 'hanging, slipping on bars of soap or falling out of windows'. Not one member of the police force had been held responsible for any of these 45 deaths. Death number 46, however, was different – the dead man was the leader of the Black

Consciousness movement, Steve Biko.

Stephen Bantu Biko was born in King William's Town in 1946. After his schooling, he studied medicine at Natal University. At first, he involved himself in NUSAS, the National Union of South African Students. The strong white liberal representation within this group soon frustrated Biko and in 1968 SASO, the all-black Students Union, was formed with Biko as its first president. He explained the reasons for the split:

> When we broke away to form an exclusive black movement we were accused of being anti-white. But with many more whites at university the non-racial students union was dominated by white liberals. They made all the decisions for us. We needed time to look at our own problems, and not leave them to people without experience of the terrible conditions in the black townships or of the system of Bantu education. ['Bantu education' was the policy of segregated education for black children. It was funded separately from white education and was vastly inferior.]

Biko spent some time touring the country explaining the concepts of Black Consciousness, in particular the meaning of the term 'black'. Black people, he argued, included all those designated 'non-white' by the state. In other words, people who had historically been oppressed because of their colour or racial background were all 'black'. Therefore, the Black Consciousness movement welcomed not only 'Africans', but 'coloureds' and Indians as well.

Biko was not only a political activist and theorist. He was deeply aware of the practical day-to-day problems that his people suffered. His response, consistent with the Black Consciousness philosophy, was to encourage self-help. To this end, he founded the Zimele Trust Fund to help political prisoners and their families, and the Ginsberg Educational Trust for assisting black students.

The Black Consciousness movement descended from the several organizations the government had banned in 1960 soon after the Sharpeville massacre – in particular the ANC and the PAC (Pan-Africanist Congress). The political and social philosophy behind the movement was not an entirely new creation by Biko and his supporters. The general principle of African unity, which Biko upheld, had also been the first aim of the ANC. It was a principle that had been put forward by the ANC Youth League in which Mandela played a leading role.

One of the other leaders of the ANC Youth League was a young Zulu man called Anton Lembede. Lembede had come to the conclusion that there was no hope for black South Africans as long as they relied on whites to liberate them. It is unfair though to compare Lembede with Biko. Lembede had prepared a policy document for the ANC which argued that co-operation between Africans and other groups should be rejected. This was not the Black Consciousness view. Lembede said the following:

> Non-European unity is a fantastic dream which has no foundation in reality.

Lembede further stated that racism had brought about a pathological state of mind among blacks. This resulted in an inferiority complex and the idolization of white values. In some respects, this particular observation had much in common with Biko's. Lembede died very young but his ideas were taken up by the PAC when it broke away from the ANC in 1958. Others in the Youth League, like Mandela, developed away from this 'Africanist' view. Their position was that all those who were prepared to struggle against apartheid forces could do so, and would be welcomed by the ANC, irrespective of colour or race.

The Black Consciousness movement suffered similar criticisms to these made against Lembede's early 'nationalist' or 'Africanist' ideas – namely, that it was

Steve Biko, leader of the Black Consciousness movement, inspired thousands of black South Africans to resist the apartheid regime.

accused of being a 'racist philosophy'. The basis of this accusation is that it appeared to some to adopt segregationist ideas in arguing that the struggle should be fought on racial lines. Biko clearly differed from the PAC policy in several respects, particularly in its definition of 'black'. There was no denying though that Biko did not welcome whites as part of the 'black' liberation struggle. Initially, white liberals were aghast at this rejection. So too, white members of the ANC and Communist Party denounced the Black Consciousness movement as being counter productive to the 'liberation movement'. These whites held the view that all resisters of apartheid should take their lead from the 'non-racial' policies of the ANC.

Biko was misunderstood by many South Africans, often purporsefully so. He angrily rejected all charges that Black Consciousness was a form of black racism. Unlike Lembede, he called for the unity of all those who had been oppressed on the basis of race or colour. His focus would always return to the problems of the deep-rooted feelings of inferiority that black people suffered. There was no point in struggling for power, he argued, if black people hadn't conquered this crippling state of mind. Black Consciousness was an attempt to raise the aspirations, the attitudes and the confidence of black people. To do this, blacks needed to develope genuine pride in their history, culture and value system. It was an internal struggle of the mind and soul which had to be won before the outward struggle for power could be achieved. The movember argued that:

> Liberation of the black man begins first with liberation from psychological oppression by himself through an inferiority complex.

It could successfully be argued, therefore, that the main objective of the Black Consciousness movement could not, by definition, allow white assistance, as whites did not suffer the same psychological burdens as blacks.

Biko was only too aware that comparisons would be made with his philosophy and that of the PAC, inspired by Lembede. The face value similarities needed to be resisted. Biko also understood the dangers of arguing the 'Africanist' line. The government had, after all, spent many years attempting to divide the various black peoples by the Bantustan (homelands) policy, and by favouring one group over the other. The Bantustan idea consisted of creating several 'independent homelands' within the borders of South Africa for each of the 'tribal groups'. The whites would rule over the rest of South Africa. Biko recognized the Bantustan policy as a shameful attempt by the whites to create a sham democracy for the blacks within their so-called 'own contries'.

The problems facing Biko were immense. The various African peoples were divided both geographically and culturally, as was the rest of the black population, which included Asians and 'Cape coloureds'. The multi-ethnicity of the South African population was never accepted by the whites as the valuable and culture-enriching asset which it is. Rather, it has been used in precisely the opposite way – to encourage the idea that the various African peoples were constantly warring and were traditional enemies. A common white retort to the suggestion that black and white in South African could live peacefully together was: 'But the blacks can't even live peacefully with each other'. Given this white view, the dangers in promoting the concept of Black Consciousness were easy to exploit. The white government spoke of the movement as an illustration of how even black politicians preferred to operate within their 'own race', and tried to use this argument to justify the existing apartheid system.

Mindful of these accusations, those who supported the ANC argued that the Black Consciousness concept went against their aims and methods. Even Biko's strategies ran counter to the ANC's. Biko preferred

Culture and Apartheid

Apartheid is just a pigment of the imagination.

(Pieter Dirk Uys, South African satirist writing in 1991 as apartheid was in the process of being scrapped.)

South Africa has many rich and varied cultures. During the apartheid years, the European influences eclipsed the dynamic black cultural tradition that was struggling to reassert itself in the townships. For many South Africans self-exile provided the only opportunity to express themselves creatively without political interference. Anthony Sampson, writing about South African literature, describes how black and white writers resisted the oppression and strict censorship of apartheid:

Creative writers defied the pressures round them, communicating with a desperate, surging need for self-expression which comes out of all kinds of places — from jails, from slum backyards, from rich white suburbs or from exiles all over the world. The writing comes out like gas through cracks in the rock, forcing its way to the surface with an energy and authenticity which can't be mistaken.

Sampson was referring to those poets, playwrights and novelists who worked under the cruel apartheid regime, and almost always against it.

Although the government subsidized the arts, the funding inevitably went into building glittering theatres that catered for exclusively white audiences. Imported writers, like Noel Coward from Britain, were the order of the day. Meanwhile, South African anti-apartheid writers performed their plays in community halls, in self-built 'alternative' theatres and on the streets. Those other actors, musicians and writers who fled into exile to make their mark on the international arts scene remained unseen and unheard by their fellow South Africans for many years. Most anti-apartheid artists spent a period of their lives in unhappy exile. Those who chose to stay in South Africa battled on against apartheid bannings, a lack of funds and demoralizing working conditions.

Although the bleak years of oppression saw the stifling of many talents, the powerful will to resist over the years still resulted in an abundant outpouring of exciting work. The final demise of apartheid saw an additional flourishing of exciting South African talent. (See the list at the back of this book for recommended books, films and musicians.)

to work 'overground', within existing legal structures, often operating through community projects. He was also a spokesman for 'non-violent' methods. This was at a time when the ANC was clearly and openly maintaining an underground 'armed struggle'.

Biko was not to be silenced by this resistance from both pro- and anti-apartheid forces. He responded by clarifying his analyses and strategy:

We are oppressed, not as individuals, not as Zulus, Xhosas, Venda, or Indians. We are oppressed because we are black. We must use that concept to unite

ourselves and to respond as a cohesive group.

He was not suggesting that all the African peoples, including Asians and 'Cape coloureds', seek a melting pot of their cultures — a common denominator of traditions, religions and languages. He understood only too well that white South Africans had always been determined to define the issue of black history, culture and language in one emotionally laden word, 'tribalism'. The tribal argument had to be continually resisted.

Biko's message was getting through, particularly to the young people who were

June 1976 saw one of the most horrific events in the history of apartheid. Students demonstrating in Soweto against the compulsory use of the Afrikaans language in black schools were attacked by police – 575 were massacred, 2,389 injured.

desperate to shrug off the bitter defeats of the 1950s and '60s that their parents had suffered at the hands of the white government. Despite Biko's insistance that Black Consciousness was at heart a non-violent movement, it soon acquired a strong militant youth following.

In 1975, the Minister of Education issued instructions that arithmetic and social studies in all 'Bantu' secondary schools must not be taught in English, but Afrikaans. This instruction was a red flag to a bull. To a large militant group of black schoolchildren this was almost a declaration of war. Afrikaans was considered to be the language of their oppressors, and they were now being forced to use it at school whether they liked it or not. English was the language used by Africans in towns, as it was also the language of industry and commerce and therefore jobs. Afrikaans, the parents and pupils argued, was the language of police,

pass offices and prisons.

By 1976, Black Consciousness had been adopted as the popular politics of the schools. In June of that year in Soweto, 15,000 pupils protested on the Afrikaans issue. Violence on a scale that had never been seen before was about to erupt. The police opened fire on the demonstrators – at the end of these protests, 575 people had been killed and 2,389 wounded.

By now, the government had realized the dangers to them of Black Consciousness, particularly in the way it had been taken up by the new young generation of blacks determined to resist apartheid subjugation. Black Consciousness leaders were quickly arrested and tried. The charges were that these leaders had conspired to:

Commit acts which would bring revolutionary change to South Africa; and had been involved in a course of

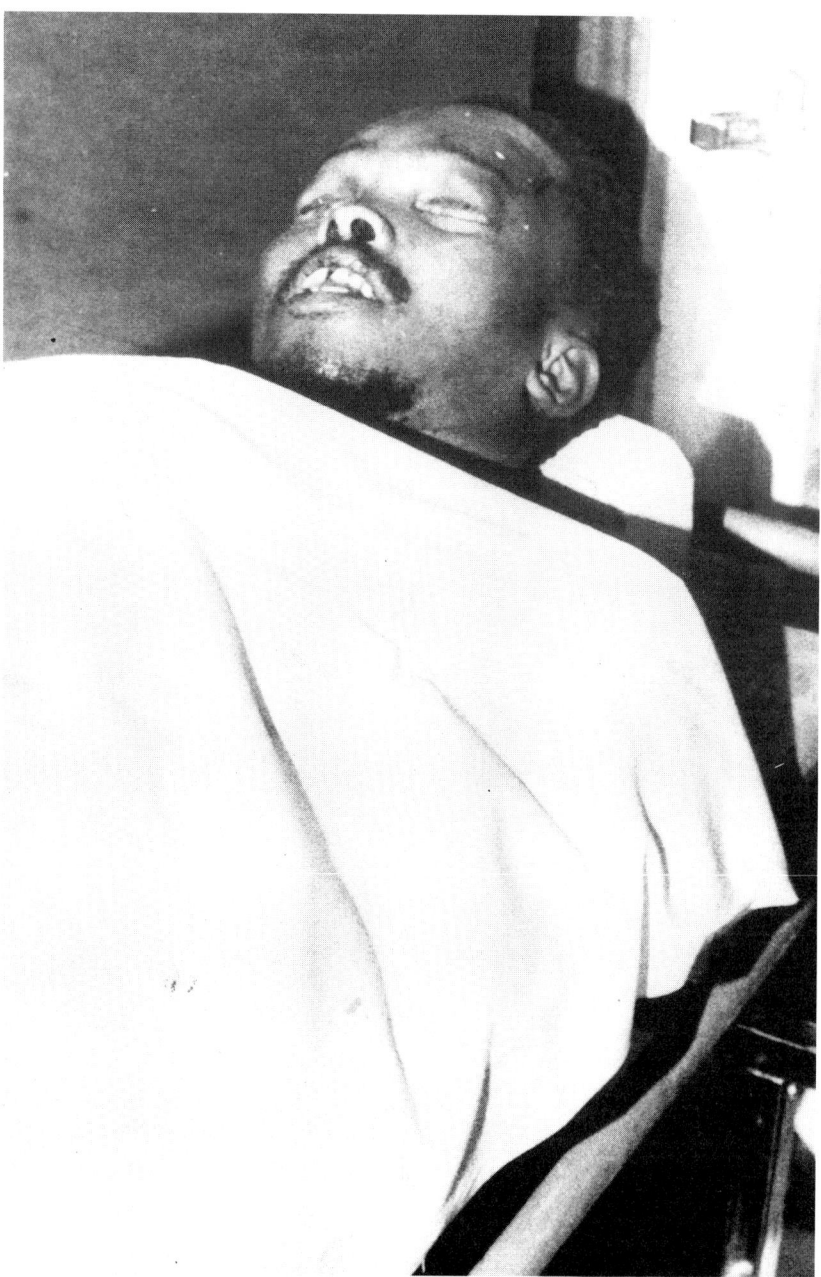

Steve Biko was murdered at the age of 31 while in police custody. The inquest into his death judged that no one was to blame. There is no way of knowing how he might have further influenced the development of anti-apartheid resistance if he had been allowed to live.

On 18 August 1977, Steve Biko was detained yet again. The police were resolved to break his spirit and rob the movement of its most inspiring leader. For 20 days he was manacled and kept naked in a cell. On 2 September, a magistrate came to see him. 'Is it compulsory that I have to be naked?' he asked. The magistrate did not reply. On 7 September he was told to dress and was interrogated, during which time he was also severely beaten. Five days later he was dead.

Two days after Biko's death, the National Party held its congress. Jimmy Kruger, the minister of justice, told his followers: 'I am not glad and I am not sorry about Mr Biko. It leaves me cold'.

The inquest that followed his death was a near farce. The verdict accepted that Biko had died as a result of a 'scuffle' with security police. According to the verdict no one was to blame. *The Guardian* newspaper in London summed up the world's response:

> The sheer perversity of the finding would cause dismay to all of black and some of white South Africa.

The Johannesburg newspaper the *Sunday Times*, in response to the verdict, challenged white South Africans:

> Now we are all accountable. The Biko inquest has served one or two useful purposes. It has exposed in chilling detail, how the system of detention operates. Nobody can plead innocence. Nobody can say, but I didn't know. Every South African must now answer to his own conscience . . . and submit to the judgement of history on his actions.

preparation to recruit blacks into a Black Power bloc hostile to whites and to the state.

Biko had already been so severely restricted that he was not charged with the group now on trial. They all received long terms of imprisonment. Biko, the acknowledged leader of the movement, was banned but still relatively free. He continued to be an inspiration to the movement, and as such he represented a threat to the apartheid state. The police were determined to stop him.

South Africa had lost a great leader. Biko was killed at the age of 31. We cannot calculate the true value of his philosophy, or contribution to the struggle against apartheid if he had lived, but we can be sure that he inspired a generation to action and resistance. Biko's death saw the beginning of a gradual decline in support of Black Consciousness. Many of the students who fled the country after the

Soweto riots left the movement and joined the ANC in exile. In the front line states they trained as soldiers in the armed wing of the ANC. By the 1990s, Biko's influence was marginal, as was the Black Consciousness movement.

Donald Woods, a white South African newspaper editor who knew Biko well, said the following:

> In the three years that I grew to know him my conviction never wavered that this was the most important political leader of the entire country, and quite simply the greatest man that it had ever been my privilege to know.

Steve Biko rejected the idea of working against apartheid within non-racial liberal groups. What were his reasons?

Do you think Black Consciousness is a racist idea?

What was the attitude of the ANC to the Black Consciousness movement?

In 1975, the government forced through a policy ordering that black schoolchildren be taught in Afrikaans. Why did this cause such a strong reaction?

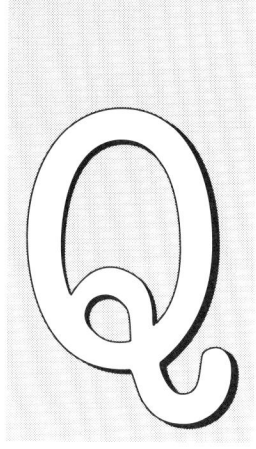

5 Reform

![Photograph of a protest march with banners reading "STATE OF EMERGENCY ...an STATE of TERROR?", "silence is TIME FOR CHANGE IS NOW", "PORT BOYCOTT", and "PROTESTING IS NOT"]

The states of emergency meant great restrictions of freedom for black South Africans as the townships were occupied by security forces. This protest march by students of the University of Cape Town was staged against the state of emergency imposed in June 1985.

The Sharpeville massacre was the culmination of resistance to apartheid that had continued throughout the 1950s. Anti-apartheid action had by now passed through various stages. As a rough guide, they are as follows.

The 1950s were a period of optimism for the black opposition. The 1960s were a decade of state repression, which ushered in a period of deep despondency. The 1970s saw the recovery of the resistance movement, despite the state of emergency and periods of gloom. (During states of emergency, the police were given wide-ranging powers to control situations which they considered threatening to public order. The authority they had to arrest and detain people would not be acceptable in any Western democracy.) During the 1980s, there was a period of large-scale violence but also of reform and, finally, genuine change.

In 1983, Prime Minister P.W. Botha offered South Africa a 'new constitution'.

The whites, coloureds and Indians would each have their own 'Houses of Assembly', of 'Representatives' and 'Delegates'. To no one's surprise the whites would retain a controlling role. The offer of 'power sharing' was clearly just a token gesture. Furthermore, the 'Africans' were to be excluded from this new constitution, but were offered a scheme whereby they could have elected local authorities in the townships.

Reverend Allan Boesak, who was 'coloured' and the President of the World Alliance of Reformed Churches, responded by saying:

> Working within the system for whatever reason contaminates you. It wears down your defences. It wets your appetite for power . . . Churches, civic organizations, trade unions, student organizations and sport bodies should unite on this issue, pool our resources, inform the people of the fraud that is about to be perpetrated in their name, and expose those plans for what they are.

Soon after that speech, Boesak gave another at a huge meeting in Cape Town. This meeting was organized to establish a united front of resistance to apartheid. There were 400 organizations in attendance, including sports clubs, nurses' guilds and political groups. The most influential organizations, however, were the trade unions, which the government had now legalized as a result of the failure of the law to suppress them. All these organizations agreed to join forces and launch the United Democratic Front. Significant among the proposals of the UDF was a clause which stated that it did not 'purport to be a substitute movement to accredited people's liberation movements'.

The message underlying this statement indicated that the UDF did not intend to replace the ANC, or to act in opposition to it. The ANC welcomed the development. Many people suspected that the UDF was a front for the still banned ANC. Most government officials said as much.

So, in response to Botha's plans for a new constitution, the opposition had organized a powerful resistance movement which proved extremely difficult to suppress. The UDF was so vast, and its membership so spread across the political and social spectrum, that the government's existing security legislation could not effectively control it.

The new 'three chamber' legislature met for the first time in September 1984. Whites, coloureds and Indians sat together in the Parliament House to the extreme anger of right-wing, pro-apartheid Afrikaners. Although the whites still retained effective control, this was a symbolic political event many of them had feared – and with good reason.

The possibility of destroying apartheid had certainly crossed the minds of many South Africans. The talk of 'reform' had signalled a crucial fact – that the white government had acknowledged its failure. Apartheid was on the way out. This offer of 'reform' was not the answer, however, but simply a means of replacing apartheid with another system designed to maintain white power and control. The 'reform apartheid' concept was never going to work, and would never be accepted.

The Sharpeville massacre in 1960 (see page 23) and the Soweto uprising in 1976 (see page 39) were huge and grave reminders to the whites that nothing less than a police state had been required to resist the growing struggle for majority rule. During both these periods, the whites responded similarly. Those who supported the government welcomed the repressive police regime that followed – convinced that only the police and army could defend their minority government. Those who rejected the killings either voiced their protest or left the country. Pessimism overtook the economy, partly because of hostile world reaction to the killings and the instability of the political situation. Property prices plummeted. Instead of the usual influx of white immigrants, 1977 and 1978 saw 3,000 net departures. Now into the 1980s, the government was to face a new form of violence that continued to hamper 'peace efforts' up to and even after Mandela's release.

The UDF had rejected Botha's reform proposals out of hand. In response, they organized successful boycotts of council elections in the black townships. At times only two or three per cent of voters who registered bothered to vote. Intimidation played a significant role in this boycott, but the electorate generally accepted the futility of accepting this token 'democratic' gesture from the government. Then on 3 September 1984, the newly elected deputy-mayor of Sharpeville was murdered. Soon, a number of other blacks accused of collaborating with the government's plans were also killed. By the end of the month 26 blacks were dead. South Africa was entering another tragic stage in the history of apartheid. Blacks were turning on those people in their own communities whom they suspected gave support to the regime.

Much of this 'black on black' violence had been organized by young people, many of whom had experienced the 1976 Soweto massacre. Deep hatred of the police, and those they considered to be police collaborators, had been instilled in them. They had not forgotten the murder of their leader Biko either. These young people, often referred to as 'comrades', decided to make the townships a no-go area for police. To a large degree this tactic worked. They were now able to attack and kill suspected 'enemies' with reduced chance of arrest. A method employed to kill 'collaborators' was to force a rubber tyre filled with petrol around the neck of a victim and set it alight. This became known as the 'necklace'.

To further enflame the situation, two quite separate organizations were developing. One of them drew its inspiration from the Black Consciousness movement and called itself AZAPO, the Azanian People's Organization. (Azania was their new name for South Africa.) AZAPO, continuing in the Africanist/ Black Consciousness tradition, refused to allow whites membership. The other organization was the UDF which was pro-ANC and opposed to AZAPO. AZAPO and UDF factions battled with each other to control various townships. Some members of the security forces welcomed this development, and often encouraged it. Black on black violence, the right wing hoped, would finally persuade the whites that the attempts to reform apartheid would never be successful, and that the system should stay as it was.

Despite this negative black response, the 'reformers' in the government were still in the majority. Some were genuinely motivated by a need to scrap apartheid. Others were merely being practical because they were aware that apartheid could not stand up to international and internal economic pressures for very much longer. The attack on white minority rule was therefore double-edged: internal black resistance and external boycotts, isolation and sanctions.

The reform package had impressed some leaders in the international community. Margaret Thatcher in the UK felt that a reward for the changes should be offered. She spoke of a 'carrot and stick' policy in which she proposed that economic sanctions be dropped. This view was rejected out of hand by South African anti-apartheid forces, and by most of the European Community. And so, white South Africans saw little material encouragement for their 'reforms'. They failed absolutely to understand that the changes they had made were largely symbolic. The main planks of apartheid were still firmly in place. The whites could not see their way ahead.

It was always a belief of pro-apartheid forces that continued minority rule could be sustained with oppressive state violence. While sectors of white nationalists could put up with this, the economy could not. And to reinforce these economic problems, the 'force' that the whites feared most of all was beginning to stir – black industrial workers were no longer afraid

Economic sanctions and consumer boycotts

Sanctions were economic measures against South Africa, usually imposed by governments. Consumer **boycotts** (the refusal to purchase South African products) were adopted by individuals. The idea behind these actions was that non-violent pressure could be put on South Africa to reject apartheid. But did they work?

The **consumer boycott** was largely unsuccessful. It relied on individuals choosing to avoid South African goods in supermarkets and shops. It did become unfashionable to purchase South African farm products. However, gold accounted for about half of South Africa's exports and this commodity was entirely unaffected by boycotts. Despite their constant efforts, anti-apartheid campaigners were constantly disappointed by the fact that between 1985 and 1990 non-gold exports from South Africa actually *rose* by 65 per cent. The effects of the consumer boycott were not seriously damaging to the South African economy.

Sanctions and **financial disinvestment** had a far greater effect. They were imposed by foreign governments, foreign companies and banks, who clearly had a great deal more power than the individuals carrying out the consumer boycotts. The sanctions were partly political, but mostly economic. As recession hit the economy and political unrest flared, international financiers began to see South Africa as a poor credit risk. Without financial investment the South African economy would soon stagnate. The investment 'pull out', together with sanctions, placed strong additional pressure on the government to scrap apartheid.

Those who argued against sanctions felt that they hurt blacks more than whites. This was a view shared by many conservatives in the West, notably Margaret Thatcher, the British Prime Minister. They also argued that sanctions and disinvestment might so damage the economy that it would be in ruins by the time apartheid was scrapped.

As more companies left South Africa, a gloom descended. Whites found it extremely difficult to purchase the consumer goods they were so used to. The psychological effect of worldwide rejection was beginning to hurt. Morale was already low due to the economic slump. The willingness to 'stand up to the world' was rapidly wearing off. White South Africans were tiring of boycotts and sanctions, and they let their government know it. Although neither the whites nor their government were prepared to admit it, sanctions and boycotts were damaging. In response to these outside pressures, reforms and changes were rapidly being made.

to use their muscle.

While the security situation could be contained for the foreseeable future, the economic crisis that was looming could not. Foreign investors were beginning to fear for their investments. Many continued to argue that their influence in the economy was a liberal one, and that they provided a useful example to South African companies when it came to wages and race relations. More often than not the facts spoke differently. Many foreign investors were in South Africa precisely to *exploit* cheap labour and the historically weak position of the workers. However, as the situation worsened they too began to pull out, arguing – after many years of profiteering from apartheid – that they now found the system immoral. The truth was that they had also lost faith in the National Party to secure their investments. The white government had only one choice – genuine reform which convincingly offered to dismantle grand apartheid.

By 1986, both Margaret Thatcher and Ronald Reagan had accepted the role that the ANC might play in a future South

After Nelson Mandela's release, he was invited by heads of state throughout the world to visit their countries. Mrs Thatcher, despite her former insistance that the ANC was a terrorist organization and her long-standing opposition to economic sanctions against the South African government, was no exception. She met Mandela in London in July 1990.

This UDF meeting was protesting against the presence of troops in townships during the state of emergency in 1986.

Africa. Until then, the ANC had been written off by both these leaders as a 'terrorist movement'. It had now become increasingly clear to most observers that the ANC might be a likely winner in the event of a nationwide election. The Western powers, including the UK and the USA, were beginning to accept this view. The pressure on Botha to release Nelson Mandela, the leader of the ANC, was growing.

To further complicate Botha's problems, many of the world's leading financiers informed him that his reforms were not sufficient to create a secure political climate for their investments. The outside world was now asking the nationalist government to negotiate a compromise with the country's black leaders. Botha knew that once he agreed to free Mandela

and sit down with him to discuss the future, the inevitable demand would be the handing over of political power to a majority government. But Botha had neither the mandate from the white electorate nor the desire to agree to this demand. His reform plans had run out of steam, and in the minds of many whites the government had lost control.

In June 1986, P.W. Botha decided that total control of the country needed to be regained before his 'reform' programme could continue. A state of emergency was declared. This was an admittance that 'reform' had failed. The word itself had been ridiculed from the outset. It was impossible to *reform* apartheid, many in opposition argued. It needed to be *scrapped*.

One of the most loathed elements of

F.W. de Klerk, described by Nelson Mandela as a 'man of integrity' was the first National Party prime minister to admit to the failure of apartheid.

apartheid, the homelands policy, was just one example of several grand apartheid concepts that Botha had insisted on preserving. The homelands policy was deeply resented. The Transkei, Ciskei and Venda homelands were already being ruled under virtual states of emergency. Millions of black South Africans had never set foot in their homelands – neither had they any wish to do so. None of the homelands was able to balance its budget and none could produce the food to feed its own population. In 1980, Parliament stated that 1.43 million people in the homelands were destitute.

Leaders of the homelands were universally condemned as 'stooges' of white South Africa. They were often the focus of black resentment, and more often the butt of white humour. Corruption in their administrations was widespread. The 'independent' homelands had no international recognition whatsoever outside South Africa. Homelands passports were not accepted anywhere except South Africa.

The South African government was forced to address this huge problem. Finally, it began to indicate a shift in thinking about the homelands – despite the huge political investment it had in the concept. Mr Botha stated that the question of citizenship was now being reconsidered. He also said that the government was committed to 'the principle of a geographically united South Africa, a common citizenship and universal franchise'.

Reformers within the National Party had finally begun to acknowledge the failure of the homelands policy. The various homelands were based on the 260 old reserves, which were scattered about the country. These areas were established under legislation passed in 1913 and 1936, which designated the restricted areas in which blacks could purchase property.

They were never the true 'homelands' of the various tribes, as was pretended. As the Commonwealth report of 1986 said:

> The lack of geographical unity gives the lie to any basis in history. One 'homeland', Kwazulu, is now a jumble of some ten jigsaw pieces – an 'archipelagic state', scattered across a continental white 'sea'.

Promises of genuine change were almost too late. Despite continued talk of change, the years of 'reform' had brought no benefits to the whites. If anything, they were more isolated than ever, and anti-apartheid forces were proving impossible to control. The black unions were also seen to be a far tougher and more organized force than the government had dared to believe. Tinkering with apartheid clearly served no other purpose than to draw closer the realization of black majority rule. And this eventuality was still not on the white agenda.

In May 1987, the white electorate predictably swung to the right, away from the reform policies of the 1980s. Botha followed them. The whites had retreated once again to their camp. Repression and apartheid had worked for them up until then, they believed, and the government was mandated to stop the reform programme in its tracks. One of their first measures was to reintroduce apartheid in Groote Schuur Hospital, a showcase institution.

But it was too late. South Africa's blacks were finally assured of their power to force change. They had at last stopped believing in the state's invulnerability and were ready to claim their rights. Their unlikely allies, world financiers, were refusing to support economic apartheid any longer. Something, or someone, had to give way. It was to be the new prime minister, F.W. de Klerk.

In 1983, the Prime Minister P.W. Botha put forward a new constitution for South Africa. Why was it rejected by the black majority?

Anti-apartheid protesters said that they were not interested in reforming the system, but instead they wanted complete change. Would it have been possible to reform the concept of apartheid?

Is there anything to be said in favour of apartheid? Can you imagine any country in the world where elements of apartheid might improve the situation?

When Mrs Thatcher spoke of a 'carrot and a stick' approach to the South African white government, what do you think she meant? Was she right?

Why were the leaders of the 'homelands' rejected by the majority of South Africans?

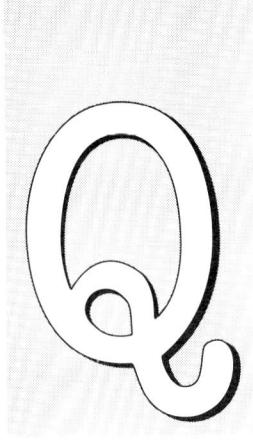

6 The Long Road to Democracy

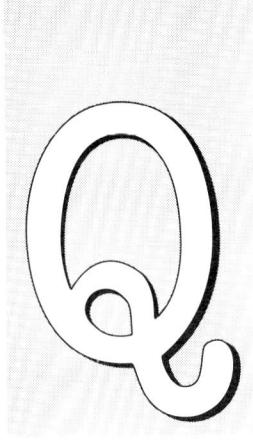

Eugene Terreblanche speaks to the members of his Afrikaner Resistance Movement (AWB) near Pretoria. The organization's emblem closely resembles the Nazi swastika and is a reminder of the dangerous fanaticism within this fascist movement.

This book began with the release of Nelson Mandela in February 1990. It was recognized at the time as now, as both a humanitarian gesture and a symbolic political act with enormous consequences. For 27 years Mandela had been silenced by the white government. Yet as each of these silent years passed his voice seemed to get louder and his message seemed to reach further. By the end of the 1980s he was the most famous prisoner in the world, and the international clamour for his release could no longer be ignored by white South Africans.

Nelson Mandela, during his stay in prison, had come to represent the essence of the struggle against apartheid. The South African government was always aware of that, and also that freeing Mandela would have to mean freedom for the remaining leaders of the black nationalist struggle. After these leaders were freed and their movements unbanned, there would be no going back. A

The AWB *Stormvalke* on training. These soldiers are preparing to fight against any future black majority government that comes to power. Their aim is to establish an Afrikaner *volksstaat* (people's state) based in the old Boer republics (the Transvaal and the Orange Free State). The AWB was estimated in 1986 to have 10,000 members.

chain of events would have been triggered which would inevitably lead to the end of apartheid. The release of Nelson Mandela was therefore one of the crucial signals by the government that it intended to embark on fundamental changes.

THE FEAR OF CHANGE

For the white prime minister, F.W. de Klerk, these decisions represented enormous dangers, more so because he was an Afrikaner and the leader of the political party that had created apartheid. When he freed Nelson Mandela, he was accused by many of his fellow Afrikaners of being a traitor to his people by beginning a process which would eventually strip them of overall political control.

Many pro-apartheid Afrikaners were appalled by de Klerk's actions and left his National Party to join the ranks of the Conservative Party. Even further to the right of these die-hard conservatives were groups of neo-fascists and self-professed racists who declared all out war on both de Klerk and the ANC (whom they still believed to be communists). These militant groups advocate violent methods and will retain pockets of support for many years to come. One of them, the AWB (Afrikaner Resistance Movement), pledged to mount military-style attacks on any future black government.

Other political forces have also come into play. There is the growth of 'black on black' violence, and much talk of a new 'third force'. (See page 56, 'Divide and rule')

SOUTH AFRICANS FACE TO FACE WITH EACH OTHER

The ending of apartheid has resulted in all South Africans having to confront each other in a totally new way. Whites had been taught for centuries to see blacks as politically naive and unable to run their own affairs. This was the propaganda the whites wanted to believe because in their eyes it gave them the excuse to maintain power over the majority. As black leaders were freed and given a public platform, the whites were abruptly faced with the prospect of seeing blacks as equals. Quite suddenly they were hearing the opinions of black leaders who were articulate and highly skilled political orators. Previously, all that white South Africans knew about black opinions was what their government told them – and although that message was crude it was effective. It was phrased like this:

> Most black leaders were communist agitators, trained and financially supported by foreign communist powers.

That style of government propaganda ran out of steam soon after Mandela was released and communism in eastern Europe was overthrown.

GLASNOST AND SOUTH AFRICA

Glasnost, the Russian concept of change which signified the end of Soviet communism, had a significant bearing on South African politics. Although southern Africa is both politically and geographically removed from eastern Europe, the impact of glasnost has been profound.

First World upheavals often have serious effects on the Third World. The two world wars and the Cold War had devastating repercussions in Third World countries. Similarly, the ending of the Cold War between West and East in the late 1980s saw the beginnings of democracy, not only throughout most of eastern Europe but in a number of African countries as well. While Europe was the political battleground of the Cold War between East and West, the Third World was where the Cold War was often fought for real. (Recent examples include the wars in Ethiopia, Sudan, Angola and Mozambique.)

THE SUPERPOWER BATTLE FOR AFRICA

Many African states since the end of colonialism have looked for aid to either the East or West. And with the aid came weapons. The West supplied them to almost anyone who claimed to be fighting communism, even if it meant propping up apartheid and other undemocratic regimes. Similarly, the communist block often kept in power tyrannical and cruel rulers, as long as they appeared to toe the Moscow Communist Party line. In both cases, the people of the countries ruled by such leaders suffered. The political, economic and social policies of these African states were determined by superpower interests and not by the real needs of their populations. The result was that these countries had no real democracy and little economic growth. Many of them became 'aid-dependent' – that is, unable to survive without huge aid programmes.

South Africa was an exception. Being a country immensely rich in raw materials and with a highly developed economy, it survived the destructive effects of the Cold War which ravaged the rest of Africa. Although front line states like Angola, Mozambique and Zimbabwe had rejected Western-style capitalism after independence, South Africa remained resolutely in the pro-Western bloc. South Africa's strategic geographical position at the bottom of Africa, and its important natural resources, made it a country that the West was not prepared to lose. White South Africans were always aware of this. In a booklet published by the white government which was intended to introduce immigrants to South Africa, this view is confirmed:

> The Republic's strategic importance to the West goes beyond its mineral wealth. The country commands the most important sea route between East and West, along which most of the West's oil supplies are carried. South Africa has always been strongly anti-communist, and during the past two decades has built up and equipped from

its own resources a Defence Force which is acknowledged to be the most powerful on the African continent.

The same booklet provided a detailed comparison between South Africa's economic achievements and the rest of Africa's failures. The government has conveniently used the turmoil in many other African states as a warning of what would happen to South Africa if it shifted its superpower allegiances towards eastern Europe (as it believed a black government would). The threat of this happening finally evaporated with the collapse of communism. Overnight, the 'communist threat' disappeared from the government's propaganda arsenal, and the likelihood of black majority rule became a reality.

THE (COMMUNIST) PARTY IS OVER

Although the ANC had been accepted by many Western nations as the legitimate voice of black opposition to apartheid, it had historical connections with the South African Communist Party (which had taken instructions from the Soviet Union, from whom it received much support.) South African whites thus had some evidence of communist influence in the ANC during the years of resistance. However, within a year of Mandela's release the communist influence within the ANC was in serious decline. By the middle of 1991, in a determined attempt to survive, the South African Communist Party announced that it was moving away from hard-line Marxism and could even see a South Africa in which private enterprise could play a useful role. The South African Communist Party was obviously shaken by what was happening in eastern Europe, and by the acceptance within the ANC of a market-based economy (free enterprise).

As the Soviet Union began to withdraw support from various African states the effect was not only felt in South Africa. In 1990 and 1991, no less than nine heads of African states fell. Together with their demise, the idea of the one-party state also

collapsed. Many African rulers after independence believed that the one-party state was the most appropriate political system for the continent. They had argued that the dangers of multi-party democracy would be political parties forming with tribal allegiances. In reality, many of the one-party African states ended up having tribal or clan allegiances anyway.

The West had brought colonialism to Africa, exploiting an entire continent, finally leaving behind a legacy of suffering and disorder. For its part, the Soviet Union sponsored so-called 'Marxist' states, which also failed Africa and robbed millions of people of a democratic voice. In addition to this tragedy, it also offered the whites of South Africa a ready-made excuse that 'African communists cannot successfully run efficient economies'. The ANC-South African Communist Party alliance only served to reinforce the whites' fears. By September 1991, with the demise of communism in the Soviet Union, that excuse for apartheid was dead and buried.

A NEW CONSTITUTION FOR SOUTH AFRICA

White South Africans claimed for decades that their system of government was democratic. In reality, it was a one-race democracy. White South Africans always accused the rest of Africa of oppressive government, but refused to acknowledge that the apartheid regime was itself not a real democracy. The evidence for this is the fact that a single party, the National Party, held onto power for over 40 years from 1948. Although the whites always described their voting system as democratic, they were totally ignoring the fact that it excluded three-quarters of the population.

By 1990 the National Party had agreed that the 'apartheid experiment' had failed, but it still refused to take the burden of blame for decades of authoritarian rule. Instead, it began to present itself as a 'reforming' party, prepared to face the ANC in an open election. The idea that the

National Party could go into a non-racial election and win seemed unthinkable – but de Klerk was moving in a direction that prompted some observers to believe that he was serious.

How could the party of apartheid hope to take on the African National Congress in a fair and open election? The ANC was bound to be supported by a huge proportion of South African blacks and many left-wing whites. De Klerk's strategy slowly became clear. The first step was to allow blacks to join the National Party. Significant numbers of black, 'coloured' and Indian people who were not pro-ANC would have to be recruited to the party. Many English-speaking whites were already supporting de Klerk. Political analysts then began to argue that a new 'Democratic Alliance' led by the National Party could win enough seats at a general election to prevent the ANC from claiming

outright victory. (The 'Alliance' would have to include the Zulu-based Inkatha organization.) In neighbouring Namibia, a few years previously, a similar 'democratic alliance' had prevented SWAPO from achieving what had seemed certain to be a landslide victory. (SWAPO was the liberation movement which had struggled for Namibian independence from South Africa.)

De Klerk placed young reformist men in his cabinet, all determined to press ahead with his gamble. Then came 'Inkathagate'.

INKATHAGATE

Inkathagate was a scandal for the government which could easily have halted the 'peace process', but in fact speeded it up. For several years, the ANC had been accusing the government of supporting Chief Buthelezi's Inkatha Freedom Party and a 'dirty tricks' campaign against ANC

'Black on black' violence became widespread in the 1980s and early '90s. This scene of devastation at Phola Park Township shows the aftermath of Zulu attacks on Xhosa houses.

Divide and rule

The 'black on black' violence that erupted during the last years of apartheid did not surprise many South Africans, despite the horrific scale of the killings. Apartheid had sown the seeds of distrust among all of South Africa's peoples, not only between black and white. The system thrived on division which was its very lifeblood. And if these 'divisions' were not deep enough then apartheid set out to drive wedges where they hardly existed before. Many methods were used. The pass laws were targeted at 'African' people but not against 'coloured', 'white' and 'Indian' people. In the Orange Free State all people were allowed to settle, except 'Indians'. 'Coloureds' and 'Indians' were given limited voting rights but not 'Africans'. In 1984, the government announced that Chinese people could claim the same status under the Group Areas Act as whites. And so it went on, the government pitching one degrading law at one group and not at the other. The result was that prejudice and resentment, jealousy and bitterness developed between the races, growing stronger day by day, decade by decade. As the rivalry between groups intensified it provided 'evidence' for the government's case that different races should be kept apart. The government conveniently forgot that its own policies had caused the rivalry in the first place.

Years of direct government effort went into 'dividing' the Zulu people from the Xhosa-speaking people. (Buthelezi, the leader of Inkatha, was a Zulu. Mandela, the leader of the ANC, was Xhosa-speaking.) If the government could show to the world that majority rule would result in inter-'tribal' warfare, particularly between Zulu and Xhosa, then, they believed apartheid would have 'proven itself worthwhile'. In this attempt they finally overreached themselves and the Inkathagate scandal was the result (see below).

The ANC claimed that something they called the 'third force' was operating to stir up 'black on black' violence. They believed that this 'force' was a conspiracy of all those whites determined to encourage violence between blacks. Many whites claimed the ANC had invented this force to blame them for the fighting in the townships. We will never know the exact make-up of this force, or how well organized it was, but Inkathagate did prove that in one form or the other it existed.

The miracle has been that after decades of apartheid there remains so much goodwill between the races. Despite the terrible scenes of carnage that the world witnessed during the scrapping of apartheid, there remained a groundswell of accord between all South Africans — even between black and white. And so, even in its principal aim apartheid was proven to have failed.

leaders. Until the government ceased these activities, the ANC argued, the peace process would be deadlocked. (See above, 'Divide and rule'.)

Inkatha had rejected almost every ANC strategy to rid South Africa of apartheid. In particular it had rejected the ANC's call for sanctions against South Africa until apartheid was ended. Naturally the white government welcomed this particular view, and the majority of South African whites looked favourably on Inkatha's leader, Chief Buthelezi. Black support for Inkatha was always relatively small, but the whites preferred to portray him as their candidate to lead South Africa's blacks. Although it was Inkatha who initiated much of the 'black on black' violence, the whites continued to blame supporters of their old enemy, the ANC.

Then in July 1991, a secret government document was leaked which disclosed that the South African security police had trained 150 Inkatha members, and that the government had supported it financially. The leak was genuine and the

Chief Buthelezi and members of his Inkatha Freedom Party. In July 1991, it was revealed that Inkatha had received funding from the government in order to weaken the ANC – the organization with the majority of black support.

government was forced to admit to it, and also to the fact that it had financed organizations determined to destabilize the ANC. Finally it was revealed that the government had influenced the elections in neighbouring Namibia. The ghosts of the worst days of apartheid had returned to haunt de Klerk. The casual use of tax payers' money to manipulate political events was taken for granted in the past, but most South Africans felt that de Klerk had rid his government of those tactics. His response was immediate. He told South Africa on a live television broadcast:

It is a fact that confidence has been shaken [in the government] and it is necessary, therefore, to restore it. Favouring only some political parties or movements from the treasury is unacceptable. All special secret projects which could have been considered to constitute support for political parties or organizations have now been cancelled.

The ANC was angry at the disclosures, but was quietly pleased that its suspicions had finally been proven correct. Furthermore, Buthelezi had been largely discredited. In the immediate aftermath of the disclosure, many South Africans expected Mandela to pull back from negotiations and let the government stew in its embarrassment. Instead, he decided to do the opposite. The ANC sensed that the scandal had offered it a critical bargaining advantage, and indicated that it wanted the process to move swiftly forward. The Inkathagate scandal therefore removed a crucial obstacle in the path towards democracy and brought the ANC and the government more quickly to the

In 1990, F.W. de Klerk and Nelson Mandela began what was to be a long process – that of deciding on a new form of government for South Africa. Here, they shake hands after three days of talks in Cape Town, May 1990.

hardest phase of negotiations – agreeing to a post-apartheid constitution for South Africa.

DEMOCRATIC RULE – WITH SAFEGUARDS?

Towards the end of 1991, the whites were suggesting models of government which would offer them a continued say in the running of the country. On the other hand, black leaders were calling for an interim government 'of national unity' to supervise a transition of power, and for one-person, one-vote elections for a new assembly. This new assembly, they claimed, would then draw up a new constitution. De Klerk rejected this. He claimed that South Africa was 'an internationally recognized government of a sovereign independent state, with an administration which had the right to stay in power through the reform process it had initiated'. His preference was for both sides to offer new ideas for a constitution, and to negotiate a compromise.

Politicians and academics have offered numerous models for these discussions. In August 1991, de Klerk finally unveiled the National Party's proposals for a new constitution. They included splitting the role of the president into a 'three to five member council of state'. A 'two-tier Westminister parliament [like the House of Commons and House of Lords in Britain] would come into being, but without group domination'. The country would also be divided into nine regions, 'each with its own government'. Almost every proposal was designed to prevent genuine majority rule. The ANC rejected the proposals outright, rightly pointing out that they would prevent any party, no matter how large its support, to command a majority of parliamentary seats.

The ANC did not display real anger at these ideas, although they fell well short of the organization's own demands. Behind the scenes, both sides quietly acknowledged that this was merely the beginning of a long process. The National Party had put forward its ideal scenario but nobody, least of all President de Klerk, expected the ANC to accept it. However, the end of apartheid was at last in sight – negotiations for a new constitution for South Africa had finally begun.

What arguments do militant Afrikaner groups use to defend their claims to supremacy? Are any of these arguments valid?

What do you think are the dangers of a country becoming 'aid-dependent'?

Some African leaders believe that a one-party system is suitable for African countries. What is their reasoning?

Can a one-person, one-vote system work in South Africa?

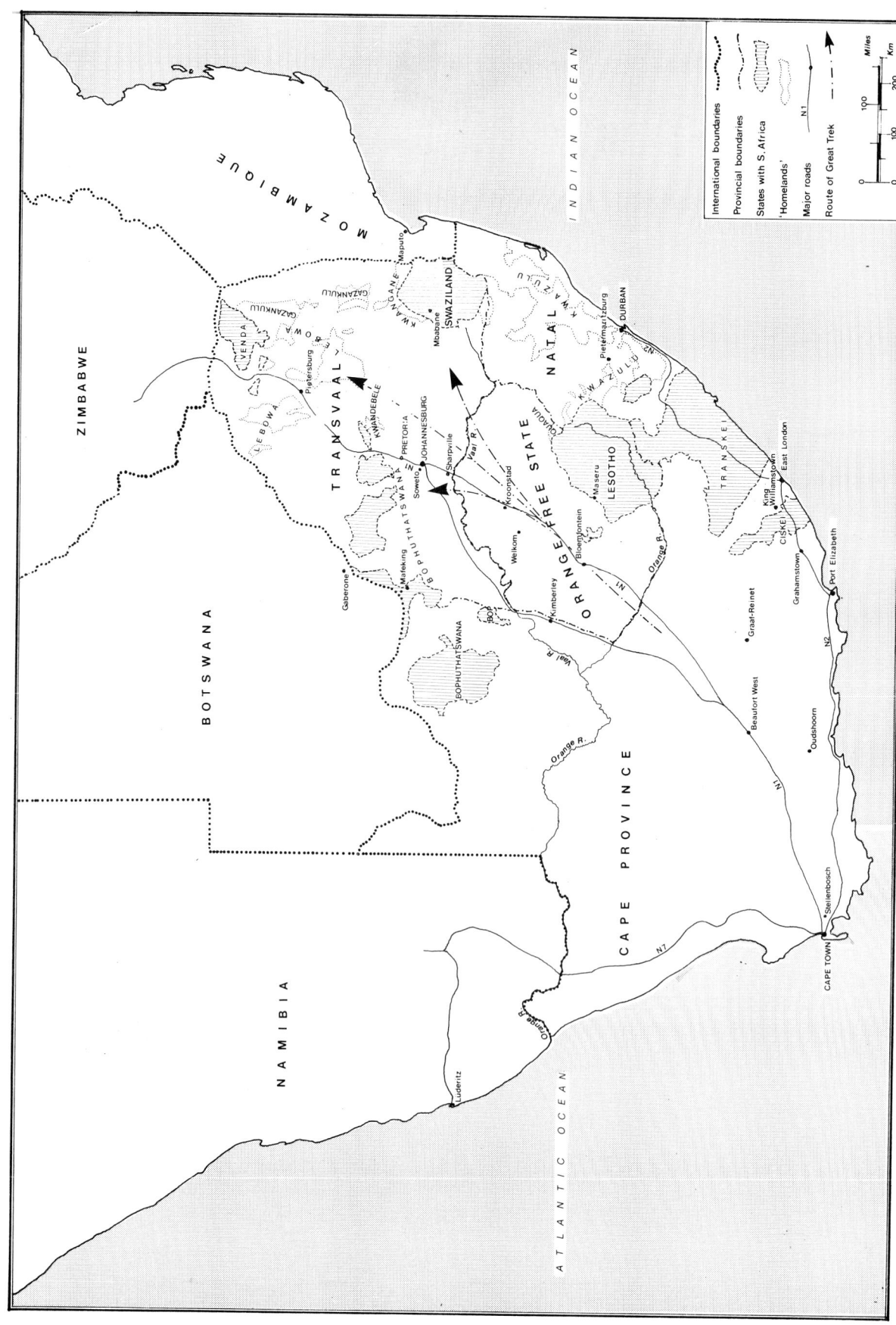

International boundaries ∙∙∙∙∙∙∙∙
Provincial boundaries
States with S. Africa
'Homelands'
Major roads ——— N1
Route of Great Trek

Miles
Km
0   100   200
0   100   200

MOZAMBIQUE

INDIAN OCEAN

ZIMBABWE

Maputo

VENDA

GAZANKULU

GAZANKULU

LEBOWA

KWANGANE

Pietersburg

SWAZILAND

Mbabane

KWANDEBELE

TRANSVAAL

KWAZULU

PRETORIA

JOHANNESBURG

Soweto

Sharpville

Vaal R.

Pietermaritzburg

DURBAN

N3

NATAL

LEBOWA

BOPHUTHATSWANA

Kroonstad

ORANGE FREE STATE

Welkom

Bloemfontein

QWAQWA

Maseru

LESOTHO

KWAZULU

TRANSKEI

King Williamstown

East London

Gaberone

Mafeking

Kimberley

N1

CISKEI

Grahamstown

Port Elizabeth

BOTSWANA

BOP

BOPHUTHATSWANA

Orange R.

Graaf-Reinet

N2

Vaal R.

Beaufort West

Oudshoorn

Orange R.

NAMIBIA

CAPE PROVINCE

N1

Luderitz

Orange R.

N7

ATLANTIC OCEAN

CAPE TOWN

Stellenbosch

60

Further Resources

SUGGESTED BOOKS

General History and Politics

Benson, M., *The Struggle for a Birthright* (IDAF, 1985)

Bernstein, H., *No 46. Steve Biko* (IDAF, 1978)

Desmond, C., *The Discarded People* (Penguin, 1970)

Jenkin, T., *Escape from Pretoria* (Kliptown Books, 1987)

Keith, I. (ed.), *It's Not Fair in Southern Africa* (Christian Aid)

Lapping, B., *Apartheid. A History* (Paladin, 1988)

Malan, R., *My Traitor's Heart* (Bodley Head, 1990)

Mandela, N., *No Easy Walk to Freedom* (Heinemann, 1965)

Marquand, L., *The Story of South Africa* (Faber, 1966)

Moss, G. (ed.), *South Africa Review* (Raven Press)

Omond, R., *The Apartheid Handbook* (Penguin, 1987)

Sikakane, Joyce, *A Window on Soweto* (IDAF, 1977)

Van Buren, L. (ed.), *New African Yearbook 1991-92* (IC)

Van Zyl Slabbert, F., *The Last White Parliament* (S & J, 1985)

Wilson, M., *A History of South Africa* (David Phillip, 1985)

It might be interesting to compare the contents of the last book with another, published by the Bureau of Information department of the South African government. It is called *This Is South Africa* (from Private Bag X745, Pretoria 0001, South Africa).

Novels, Plays and Photographic

The following is a recommended list of South African creative writers:

Adam Small, Alan Paton, Alex La Guma, Athol Fugard, Dan Jacobson, Dennis Brutus, Doris Lessing, Ezekiel Mphahlele, Hilda Bernstein, Laurens Van Der Post, Lionel Abrahams, Mary Benson, Nadime Gordimer, Oswald Mtshali, Peter Magubane (photographs), Roy Campbell.

Films

(Most of these are available on video)

Cry Freedom
A Dry White Season
Boesman And Lena
A World Apart
The Biko Inquest
The Dumping Grounds (Granada Television)
Apartheid (Granada Television Series)
The White Tribe of Africa (BBC, 1985)
South Africa: A Land Divided (This video can be borrowed from Christian Aid)

Musicians

Miriam Makeba
Amandla Album (Traditional songs. IDAF)
Dudu Pukwana

61

Date List

1000-1800 There is a gradual movement of Bantu-speakers southwards.

1487 Portuguese traders, rounding the Cape, come across the Khoikhoi people.

1590s News of the virtues of Table Bay as an excellent supply post spreads among ships' captains.

1652 Dutch settlement established in the Cape. The settlers meet and come into contact with the Khoikhoi, who supply them with meat. Jan Van Riebeeck sets up a permanent post at Cape Town. (He was employed by the powerful Dutch East India Company)

1688 Two hundred Huguenots arrive in the Cape after an outbreak of religious persecution in France.

1702 Forty-five Afrikaners ride east, 25 miles from Cape Town, and launch the first recorded battle between white and Xhosa.

1789 Beginning of the French Revolution.

1795 First British occupation of the Cape.

1800 By now Van Riebeeck's 70 settlers had increased to 20,000.

1807 Britain passes a law to outlaw the trade in slaves throughout the British Empire, which now includes the Cape Colony.

1809 British administration introduces the first 'Pass Laws', controlling the movement of black people in the Cape.

1815 As the Napoleonic Wars end Britain retains the Cape.

1820 Britain encourages 5,000 Britons to travel to and settle in the Cape.

1836-7 Six thousand Afrikaners set out on the Great Trek.

1852 Britain hands independence to Afrikaners in the Transvaal and the Orange Free State.

1854 The Trek is completed. One-quarter of the white population had left the Cape Colony.

1860 Indian labour is imported to work on the sugar plantations in Natal.

1867 Discovery of diamonds.

1881 Battle of Majuba (Transvaal burghers win back their independence).

1882 Kruger is elected president of the Transvaal.

1886 First of the big gold finds in the Transvaal.

1890 Cecil John Rhodes becomes prime minister of the Cape Province.

1895 Jameson Raid.

1899 The British cabinet sets a fleet of ships on course to the Cape. The second, and main, Boer war between the British and the Boers begins.

1902 Boer War ends. Peace of Vereeniging.

1910 The Union of South Africa is established with Louis Botha as its first prime minister.

1912 The African National Congress and the National Party are formed.

1913 The Native Land Act is passed. 7.3% of the land is set aside for 'native reserves'.

1914 Outbreak of the First World War. South Africa fights on the side of Britain.

1915 South Africa 'conquers' South West Africa and takes over administration of the territory (now known as Namibia).

1922 Two hundred whites are killed during a large strike of white miners on the Rand.

1923 The Native Urban Areas Act is passed.

1925 Afrikaans becomes the second official language (replacing Dutch).

1934 The United Party is formed.

1939 Beginning of the Second World War. Smuts takes over as prime minister after a split in the cabinet on the neutrality issue (many Afrikaners support Germany).

1945 End of the Second World War. United Nations Charter.

1948 The National Party wins the 'apartheid election'.

1949 Prohibition of Mixed Marriages Act passed.

1950 Suppression of Communism Act passed (which ironically boosted communist activity in the ANC).
Group Areas Act and **Populations Registration Act** passed.

1951 Bantu Authorities Act passed.

1952 The Defiance Campaign begins. Nelson Mandela and 19 others face trial for leading the Defiance Campaign.

1955 'Congress of the people' is held in Kliptown to adopt the 'Freedom Charter'.

1956 The Treason Trial begins.

1958 Dr Verwoerd becomes the prime minister.

1960 Sharpeville massacre. The ANC and PAC are made illegal.

1961 The Treason Trial defendants are acquitted. Albert Luthuli is awarded the Nobel Peace Prize.

1963 South Africa is expelled from the Olympics.

1966 B.J. Vorster become prime minister.

1971 Bantu Homelands Constitution Act passed (which empowers the government to offer successive 'Bantustans' self-government').

1972 Bophuthatswana and Ciskei become partly independent. The Black Consciousness movement gains support amongst black youth.

1973 Black workers strike in Natal.

1974 Violence breaks out in the mines as black workers complain about conditions of employment. Mozambique is given its independence following a revolution in Portugal.

1975 The Minister of Education decrees that arithmetic and social studies be taught in Afrikaans (in 'Bantu' secondary schools). Angola, another ex-Portuguese colony, gains independence.

1976 June 1976 Soweto riots. The Black Consciousness movement has massive support among young blacks.

1977 Steve Biko is killed by the police.

1978 P.W. Botha becomes prime minister.

1980 Following the Lancaster House Agreement in London, elections are held in Zimbabwe, bringing Mr Mugabe to power.

1983 The United Democratic Front is formed to resist apartheid. Many argue that it is a front for the ANC.

1984 The Deputy-Mayor of Sharpeville is killed, marking a new phase of 'black on black' violence. Targets are those blacks suspected of collaborating with the white government.

1985 Prime Minister Botha offers Mandela freedom if he agrees to restrict his anti-apartheid activities on his release. Mandela turns down the offer.

1986 Prime Minister Botha imposes a state of emergency.

1987 Mandela has been in prison for 25 years.

1989 F.W. de Klerk succeeds President Botha as National Party leader, and then as prime minister.
October: the ANC Secretary General, Walter Sisulu, is released.

1990 2 February: President de Klerk makes a landmark speech legalizing 33 opposition groups, including the African National Congress.
16 February: Nelson Mandela is released.
April: Inkatha and ANC supporters clash.

1991 De Klerk abolishes most apartheid legislation. Negotiations between de Klerk and Mandela continue. 'Black on black' violence escalates, but the 'Inkathagate' scandal points to the existence of a 'third force' committed to fuelling the problem. The government announces its new 'dispensation' for South Africa. The ANC rejects de Klerk's plan and proposes an interim government to replace the existing white administration. De Klerk, Mandela and Buthelezi sign a peace agreement.

Index